The Human Values
A Voyage from "I" to "We"

About the authors

Madan Lal Dewan (Ph.D., Cornell, 1948), a soil scientist and watershed management expert by profession and a veteran Rotarian, has a distinguished career as an international Civil Servant with Food and Agricultural Organization.

A very dedicated social worker, he has been working with and for the people of Uttarakhand and the Himalayas for the last 25 years. Dr. Dewan has done significant work at policy level. He was the Visiting Professor and Coordinator of Himalayan Eco System Programme with Centre for Policy Research, New Delhi and member of The National Land Use and Conservation Board of Government of India, 1984-87. He is the founder of HIMCON. He has given lead to Action Program by students, volunteers, farmers and farm women for tree planting, water harvesting & watershed management program. He has established a centre in Himalayas. People's Participation and Rejuvenation of Himalayas Environment, Uttaranchal Vision and Action Program and 15 other books are amongst his published works. He has co-authored with Prof. M.R. Chilana a book "Human Value: A Task for All". He is President of Mountain India People Forum (MIPF) and also President of Global Warming Reduction Centre (GWRC).

Ashok Kini Hosdurg, born in the divine abode of great saints Swamy Nityananda and Swamy Ramdas in Kanhangad, his love towards Mother Earth and all her inhabitants was visible from his unique actions as a child. Graduated from Calicut University, he started his career as an Army Officer in the Indian Army. He served as a soldier of peace in Nagaland, Indian Peace Keeping Force in Sri Lanka and United Nations Peace Keeping Mission in Angola. He was awarded Sena Medal for distinguished service during Kargil war. He was also awarded Vishisht Seva Medal for his devotion to duty. He was awarded "Distinguished Fellow" by Manipal University for Hospitality. Popularly called as "Divine Colonel" for his spiritual bent of mind, Kini has been giving spiritual counselling to all sections of people since 1998.

He was awarded Sewa Ratna award by Swamijee of Kanchi Kama Koti Pitham for his service to humanity in 2005. He is founder of "SAVE HIMALAYA—SAVE EARTH" mission.

Pradeep Nayak, a Mathematician by training and an Animation Filmmaker by choice, is in the field of communication since 1993. He started his career as a cartoonist for the weekly "The Sun". After a brief stint he joined "The Indian Council of Social Marketing" as a Communication Designer, where he had made significant contributions to various social marketing projects on Primary Health Care. Since 1999 he is involved in making animation films. Based in Mumbai, his organisation "TAMASHA"—a Treasure of Animated and Mannered Shapes.

His collaboration with Dr. M.L. Dewan, an honorary member of the Indian Council of Social Marketing, dates back to 1995. Both share the common interest of their "Love for Himalayas" other than education, healthcare and Human Values for people's upliftment everywhere with special reference to children, citizens of tomorrow.

The Human Values
A Voyage from "I" to "We"

M.L. Dewan
Ashok Kini Hosdurg
Pradeep Nayak

FAITH FOUNDATION

Published by

CONCEPT PUBLISHING COMPANY, NEW DELHI-110 059

Cataloging in Publication Data—DK
Courtesy: D.K. Agencies (P) Ltd. <docinfo@dkagencies.com>

Dewan, M. L. (Madan Lal), 1922-
The human values : a voyage from "I" to "we" / M.L. Dewan, Ashok Kini Hosdurg and Pradeep Nayak.
p. cm.
ISBN 13: 9788180695537
ISBN 10: 8180695530

1. Values—Study and teaching. 2. Ethics. 3. Self-knowledge, Theory of. 4. Fables. I. Hosdurg, Ashok Kini, 1962- joint author. II. Nayak, Pradeep, joint author. II. Title.

DDC 303.372 22

ISBN-13 : 978-81-8069-553-7 (H.B.)
ISBN-10 : 81-8069-553-0 (H.B.)

First Edition 2009

Published and Printed by
Ashok Kumar Mittal
Concept Publishing Company
A/15-16, Commercial Block, Mohan Garden
NEW DELHI-110059 (India)
Phones : 25351460, 25351794
Fax : 091-11-25357103
Email : publishing@conceptpub.com

DR. KARAN SINGH
MEMBER OF PARLIAMENT
(RAJYA SABHA)
CHAIRMAN
COMMITTEE ON ETHICS

Office : 127, Parliament House Annexe,
New Delhi-110 001
Ph. : 2303-4254, 2379-4326
Fax : 23012009
E-mail : karansi@sansad.nic.in

Foreword

Dr. M.L. Dewan, apart from being a noted environmentalist who has done valuable work for Himalayan conservation, is also a humanist and deeply interested in value based education. In this context he has prepared this book *Human Values : A Voyage from 'I' to 'We'*, jointly with Ashok Kini Hosdurg and Pradeep Nayak, in which they have included interesting anecdotes and examples of positive values such as peace, love and non-violence, truth and right action.

This book will surely be useful to educators, parents and many others dealing with children including social workers. The whole concept is to move from the individual ego attachment to a broader commitment to the welfare of society. As the Sanskrit saying goes, our goal should be आत्मनो मोक्षार्थं जगत हिताय च – While we must work for our individual spiritual liberation we must at the same time fulfil our responsibilities and repay our debt to the society, to create an enlightened Global Society.

I commend this book to the general public.

Karan Singh

1 August 2008

Karan Singh

Note from
Faith Foundation

Value based education is the urgent need of today in India, for humanity is confronted with a crisis of character and culture. The human values which were our backbone of culture have declined in the recent past and in all spheres of life. Erratic behaviour of children in schools and horrifying criminal acts of youth in public and also in the broad daylight are enough indicators to all of us, that our society is loosing human values. Our dream of living in a secured, protected and peaceful world will become a reality only if we collectively hold on to the human values and imbibe them in our students, youths and future generation.

The future of our country depends on our youth, the students in schools and colleges for whom therefore specially and also for all other sections of people, education in human values is a must. Ancient India always promoted a theory and practice of living together called "VASUDEVA KUTUMBAKAM" which was value based one world family.

The book, The Human Values, A Voyage from "I" to "We", with its appropriate and inspiring contents on human values is specially prepared for students and youths. We are human beings. We have therefore formulated human values to live in harmony in the society. By observing them, we foster them. They in turn promote harmonious co-existence of all of us in the Global Society. Education in human values retains the humanness in us, promotes purity in us and thereby helps us to unfold the divinity in our inner self. In the process we build our good character.

Faith Foundation is therefore happy to co-sponsor this publication for the service of the students and youths of our great nation with a hope and with the faith, that the younger generation and also people at large will benefit from gaining the knowledge by reading this book. It is an attempt by us to create an Enlightened Global Society to preserve and protect ancient Indian culture and to march towards creating one world family.

We are happy to pen down some important human values in this book form.

We congratulate you for keeping your hands on this book A Voyage from "I" to "We". The journey from darkness to the eternal light is for sure long but fascinating all the way. This book for sure will help us all immensely. Although the book is written in the context of "children" or "students" it definitely is meant for all of us. Happy voyage.

Any suggestion for improvement of the book will be warmly welcomed.

FAITH FOUNDATION
NEW DELHI-110024
www.faithfoundation.in

Preface

Ever since man came into existence good and healthy living has been his prime concern. The experienced always shares his experiences and observations among the next generation.

It's also a fact that nobody likes advices. It's so obvious! Nobody likes to see a naked person because it is not a pleasant view. We cover ourselves with clothes so that we look presentable. Similarly just plain advices seem very rude and irritating. Isn't it? That's why the wise coated them with interesting fables and stories, so that we'd enjoy the stories and get the advice as well.

Let us start with a nice story:

Once Adolph Hitler, the infamous dictator, went to an old rabbi (the Jewish wise man), and said to him, "I have heard that you are a great mystic. Can you help me have a revelation from God? Otherwise I will kill you." The rabbi said "Of course! This very moment it can be done. You just go outside, stand on the street."

Hitler said, "But it is raining".

"Don't be worried. You stand in the rain for fifteen minutes and look at the sky, and there will be a revelation!"

Hitler grumbled, "Remember, if no revelation happens I am going to kill you."

"Have a try. It always happens. It has never failed me," the rabbi encouraged him.

Hitler went out and stood there as instructed. He came back thoroughly soaked. "Look at me," he wailed. "I didn't get any revelation, I only felt like a blithering idiot."

"Not bad," chuckled the rabbi. "Don't you think that was quite a revelation for a first try?"

More or less we all live inside our self-made images. We must first try and break it so that we understand from a different perspective what positive human values mean to us.

Before proceeding further we must objectify certain emotions.

The five emotions that degrade the human being are:

1. Lust (Kama)
2. Anger (Krodh)
3. Greed (Lobh)
4. Attachment (Moh)
5. Ego (Ahankar)

And the five qualities that are responsible for human triumph are:

1. Truth (Satya)
2. Nonviolence (Ahimsha)
3. Peace (Shanti)
4. Right Action (Sat-karma)
5. Love (Prem)

Ancient Indian aesthetic though codified our emotional responses to life into nine separately distinguishable categories.

1. Shringara (erotic love)
2. Karuna (compassion)
3. Adbhuta (Awe, wonderment)
4. Shant (Peace, equanimity)

5. Hasya (Laughter, mirth)
6. Veer (valour, heroism)
7. Bhaya (fear)
8. Vibhatsa (disgust)
9. Raudra (anger, fury)

These nine rasas or sentiments are the gist of our emotional lives. For, at all times, we are feeling one or the other of these emotions - we are reacting in the emotional language of the rasas. Literally, rasa is essence, the juice of life. As we begin our journey into this world, one of the first things we do is to populate our world with rasas.

Avoid Negative Emotions

As the negative and positive emotions are distinct as mentioned above let us handle our emotions effectively. Do you know effective handling of emotions holds the key to Health and Happiness?

By ignoring this aspect, we not only jeopardize our health, but also deprive ourselves of the fountainhead of bliss that lies hidden within.

Dr. Alexio Carrel, winner of the Nobel Prize for Medicine, had said, "Emotions determine the contraction or dilation of the small arteries and are accompanied by changes in the circulation of blood. Envy, hate and fear, when become habitual, are capable of starting organic changes and diseases. Protracted sorrows and constant worry prepare the way for the development of cancer."

Sages and scriptures have prescribed the triad of Faith, Persistence and Prayer to overcome negative emotions. The Bible says, "If you have faith, nothing is impossible unto you." The need is to learn to convert mere belief into unflinching faith, unshaken by the severest blows of life. Evidence shows that God does not let anyone enjoy fruits without passing the test of persistence.

We must learn to communicate with God just as we do with our Parents.

Antonio and Sylvie Craxi spent ten years living in Southern India at Shri Shri Satya Sain Baba's Ashram, absorbing Hindu philosophy, practices and principles.
In 1985 the Craxi's worked together to carefully craft such a reduction of the Vedanta philosophy, which they termed as "Human Values A Voyage from I to We". The Craxi's incorporated children's literature such as the `Panchatantra' and asked well-known Italian illustrators to reinforce their message into a more articulate visual

language. It took two years, from 1985 to 1987, to do so. Finally, the exhibition took place in Milan, on the 4th of November 1987.
This book has already been published in Italian, French, English, Portuguese and Greek.

We are glad to say that Mr. Craxi very willingly & affectionately did give his permission to Indianize it & get it published in English or Hindi & any other Indian languages.

Five Human Values mentioned in the "Human Values - A Voyage from I to We" which we are presenting here in the form of fables & Stories will, we trust, help our readers of all ages to adapt and have a useful voyage from I to We, also in prayerful communication with God.

Dr. M.L. Dewan
Ashok Kini Hosdurg
Pradeep Nayak

Acknowledgements

Most grateful thanks to Mr. Antonio Craxi and Ms. Sylvia Craxi, an Italian couple who spent some years with Shri Shri Satya Saibaba at Prasanthi Nilayam, in Puttaparthy, Andhra Pradesh and experienced "Human Values" in practice. They decided to present it in a book form, gave it a methodology, a character and the book was dedicated to all the children of the world.

To Mr. Craxi, we phoned and asked him to give us permission to learn from their excellent publication and to Indianise the stories and write up. He very willingly and affectionately did give us the permission, but unfortunately passed away soon. Thereafter we sent the copy and then asked his wife Sylvia through the publishers "PERSONA" hoping that she is living and get this acknowledgement and thanks from us. However, we know that they were not looking for or waiting for any thanks. Thanks to his or their souls.

Thanks to Shri Shri Satyasai Baba Centre where the Craxis got the inspiration from and prepared the wonderful document in Human Values and called it a Voyage from "I" to "We".

Grateful thanks to Dr. Karan Singh for writing such a kind, wonderful inspiring Foreword to this book.

Warm thanks to Prof. M.R. Chilana who is a man of "Human Values" and has served in National Council of Education Research and Technology (NCERT) on promoting and teaching about Human Values. His first co-authoring on "Human Values - A Task for All" has opened new avenues for practice of Human Values to all the citizens of India and to the world.

Thanks are due to Mr. Ambrish Beniwal and Mr. Sharad Govindan, the colleagues of co-author Pradeep Nayak who helped us in design and illustration of this special book.

Special and Grateful thanks to Dr. S.Y. Quraishi, IAS, the founder Chairman of the Indian Council of Social Marketing for bringing us together and stimulate us in preparation of this book and the preparatory work for it.

Thanks to the brain behind the book, Dr. M.L. Dewan and Pradeep Nayak.

Collaborative thanks to Lt. Col. Ashok Kini, SM, VSM, former Comptroller for Rashtrapati Bhavan, and now founder member of Faith Foundation, who is always deeply interested in Spiritualism and Human Values not only for the children of India but for the entire world.

Thanks to Ms. Nisha Chaturvedi for helping us in reading the script and doing editorial corrections and improvements.

Also thanks to Ms. Rema Muraly for helping us in typesetting and documenting the manuscript.

Heartfelt thanks are due to PDG Manjit Sawhney and late Admiral Ramesh Bhalla for promoting the principles and steps for Human Values—A Voyage from "I" to "We" in the Rotary International System for Welfare of the Human kind.

We thank Gangadhara Kini H, Rishi Dhanuka and Nikhil Bhatia of Mumbai for their support in publishing this book.

Many books and publications have been utilized for preparation of this document. Our grateful thanks to all the publishers and authors of the books and publications.

We thank you readers that this book is in your hands and that you will understand what we want to communicate to you through this book.

Last but not the least our heartfelt thanks to Mr. Ashok Kumar Mittal, Chairman, Concept Publishing Company, New Delhi for undertaking this special publication.

Faith Foundation
New Delhi-110 024
www.faithfoundation.in

Contents

Love in words is truth.
This is the TRUTH 1.4

Teaching Value

When the truth hurts the intimate sentiments of each one of us it is better not to express it or find a more suitable way of expressing it.

Do you know who the astrologers are? They are the people who thrive on credulity, fear and human superstition. Those who believe in astrology, in fact have no faith on themselves and their capability.

Kundan Babu was a part time astrologer. He predicted people's futures, but did not take any money from any body for that. He claimed that he always tells the truth even if it is harsh. That's why people respected him.

Of course Kundan babu's motives were clear. Money he got from his job and astrology fetched him respect and power. What else does one need?!

One day Ramesh, a well-off person in the town came to him to know his future. He did not have any child. Kundan babu told him that he would have a child soon. And he had a son after a year!

Ramesh was too happy and thought it was Kundan babu's prediction. He went to him with lots of fruits and sweets, and requested him to predict the future of his son. Next day at Ramesh's home his wife, his mother and he eagerly looked at Kundan babu while he was studying the cute hands of the baby.

Confident with his previous prediction, Kundan babu told them that their son's fate lines show his ill health in future and probably death. Hearing such harsh words his wife and his mother became distressed and started crying. Ramesh, agitated, slapped him hard for predicting such bad things and threw him out of his house.

Confused and harassed, Kundan babu went away wandering where he went wrong.

Now isn't it obvious that whoever is born will die. Poor Kundan babu had said 'in future', but he had not said immediate future. Future can be a 100 years!

The point here is that the truth, which offends, is never the truth.

The truth must contain the following two elements: love, that is respect for others and usefulness, that is it must contribute to improve the situation or the individual.

Let's take another example. When your friend tells you that your nose looks mean and ugly, how do you feel? You just avoid talking to him or her. Instead, if he or she tells you that your eyes are beautiful and very attractive how would you feel? You certainly won't miss a chance to meet him or her everyday. Supposing both the facts about your face are true, why do you prefer latter? Because it reflects your friend's love and respect for you.

Manish's teacher scolded him "you are a lazy lump!" because he did not do his homework. Do you think his teacher is telling the truth according to the criteria of human values?

Yes! It was meant to hurt him so that he becomes more punctual. In this case Manish knows that his teacher says so for his betterment. When parents and teacher scold us it is meant to improve us and it does not wound us in our profound sentiments because it was said with love.

When it is a case of an irreparable situation remember the old but always valid proverb "silence is golden".

Teaching Objective

Human relations, solidarity, generosity, charity and altruism.

Personality Test

- Did you ever notice you have said truths that offend directly or indirectly someone?
- Have you ever tried to find the best way of expressing a truth?
- Have you ever hidden a truth by telling a lie for the fear of offending some one?
- How do you feel when someone rebukes you and lists your defects?
- Do you often make complements to someone in order to flatter them even if these are not true?

Questions

a. How do you think astrology benefited Kundan babu?
b. Why did Ramesh beat Kundan Babu?
c. What would you do if you were in his place?
d. What are your reactions when your friend harshly tells you some of your shortcomings?
e. What are your reactions when your friend appreciates your goodness?
f. Is it right on the part of a teacher to reproach you for being lazy or unwilling?
g. Does the reproach help to improve yourself even if it hurts?

Carry out this Exercise

Give several examples, drawn from your own experience, of truths said which do not represent a human value.

You reap what you sow.
This is the TRUTH 1.5

Teaching Value

The good and the bad depend on you.

Here is a story from the deserts of Rajasthan. Deep inside the desert, near an oasis lived a lonely old couple. They ran an inn. The travelers spent the nights there relaxing after a hectic journey through the sand; and their camels quenched their thirst in the cold water from the oasis.

The couple was very accommodating and cheerful. The guests therefore enjoyed their night's halt at this beautiful place.

There was only one serious danger! If a guest was rich, in the middle of the night the couple murdered him and threw him into a deep dark well at a secret place. Then they took away all his money. Nobody would get any hint of it.

YOU REAP WHAT YOU SOW

What did they do with all this money in the middle of the desert where nothing was available? They just saved for their only son, who was staying in the city.

They had sent their son to a distant relative in the city when he was just a small boy. With years of hard work and sincerity he grew up as a tall, handsome young man. Also he had earned a lot. Now a rich man, he was in love with the most beautiful girl of the town.

The girl's father, quite rich and a gentleman, wished to make a formal proposal to the boy's parents; and they decided upon an auspicious date for their engagement. He thought of giving a pleasant surprise to his parents who had not seen him since he was a small boy.

As per the plan, the boy, posing as a rich businessman, started one day ahead of his fiancée and her father. When he reached his home after two days, he was very exited and was tremendously happy to see his parents doing well. But they could not recognise him at all.

They had lots of talk until late in the night, sitting besides the fireplace. He kept on listening while both of them talked about their loving son, and how long they are waiting to see him. In his turn he told them about his life and his days in the city without revealing his identity.

The only mistake he did was to show them his moneybags; his earnings of the lifetime.

Tired of journey and in the safety of their home, he retired for a good night's sleep; and started snoring immediately.

The couple were waiting just for this moment. They had never seen so much of money before. Only this one murder, and their son would never have to work all his life!

Within no time his father's experienced hands slit his neck neatly, his mother wrapped the body without a single stain of blood, and in the darkness of the night they disposed the body without any hint.

By the time they finished counting the money it was eight o'clock in the morning.

The bride and his father arrived an hour later. After a refreshing cup of tea he told them his daughter's willingness to marry their son and asked for their permission.

Who would deny such a beautiful girl as a daughter in-law?!

Happy and surprised, they gave their consent immediately, "but you see, our son is in the city. Why did you strain yourself and your daughter by coming here? Only an ass would deny the hand of such a lovely girl." Now her father disclosed their son's identity,

"No sir. He is home; at your feet! Just call your yesterday's guest. I thought you would recognise your own blood!"

His mother was shocked, "but he said he was..."

"Oh yes! We had planned to give you a surprise. Now just call him...", he could not wait any longer.

....The old man and his wife now realized what they had done; and whom to blame for that?!

They just looked at each other without any expression, went into the house and bolted the door from inside. The clueless bride and her father remained standing there watching the fresh blood that had started flowing through the doorway.

What does the story tell?

Act justly, think rightly, and be good is the right road to avoid hasty surprises for the future. Just get one thing clear: if you put a lemon seed in the ground, no amount of sunshine, water or fertilizer would make it into an orange tree.

Teaching Objective

Self-analysis, the law of consequences, the sense of logic, rigorous internal honesty.

Personality Test

- Did you ever note that when you do something evil this comes back upon you in another way? Why?
- Why according to you, is it dangerous to cultivate bad thoughts in your mind?
- Have you ever thought that every thought, every word and every action generate reactions? Try to analyse this observation.
- Do you believe that if you act well the others will also act well?

Questions

a. What did you learn from the story?
b. The boy died because of whose fault?

c. If you sow a lemon seed can you hope that an orange tree will grow?
d. If you do a wicked action can you expect something good in exchange? Why?
e. If you do good can you receive ill in return? Why?
f. Do you prefer keeping company with companions who do good? Why?

Carry out this Exercise

Give an example of the law of nature regarding consequences.

Everything is visible to the mind's eyes. This is the TRUTH 1.6

Teaching Value

Nobody knows since when they had become pals. But I am seeing them together since the day I came here, to this town. Nobody knows their names as well, and nobody needed to know. They just called the blind man "Andha" and the paralytic, "Langra". Keeping company one with the other they were able to makeup for their physical deficiencies.

One day they were returning from another town not very far. Andha was carrying Langra on his shoulder and Langra was guiding him. After traveling quite a distance they felt hungry and thirsty as well.

ANDHA & LANGRA

Langra could see an abandoned field full of watermelons. "Look what nice watermelons are there in the field! Let's go and eat them!" He exclaimed.

But Andha did not move, "wait a moment!" he said, "first see if there is a fence around the field!"

Langra checked around the field and did not find one.

"Then see if there is a watchman around!"

Replied Langra - "No, I really don't see anyone at all. Let's go!"

Still Andha did not move. Langra insisted and then the blind man reproved him saying: "Why do you want to eat watermelons that are protected neither from animals nor people? If they had been good, don't you think that someone else would have picked them?"

Who has seen in this case? Andha or langra? And with what means did Andha succeed in seeing? With the interior eyes of his intelligence!

And these eyes do not need external light source to see anything; just like our dreams. When we see a dream our eyes are closed, but when we wake up we feel as if the incident happened just in front of our eyes.

What does this mean? There is more to see than what our open eyes can see. We must understand this truth, and always look beyond what we see with our open eyes.

Let's get into the names now! When we started this chapter we identified the blind man by calling him "Andha". But after this story our perception of Andha has changed. Now we know him as an intelligent person, who can judge with his senses.

Therefore this man has two personalities! One that is of outer appearance and the other, of his intellect or his mind.

Yet there is another personality that is what he considers himself to be!

There is "I" !

If you ask Andha about himself, what would he say?
"I am Andha and I am intelligent."

What does this mean? He considers himself as "I" and he thinks his body and his mind are part of "I".

When we say "I am Kalpana" or "I am Salmaan", we can consider that Kalpana or Salmaan are the names given to "I". Before someone gave me that name who was "I"? I was "I"!

Isn't it fascinating that Kalapana says I am kalpana, Salman says I am Salman, Andha says I am Andha and we all say I am so and so! Therefore "I" is present in every one of us! And we cannot see "I" with our open eyes.

Then who is the real I?

Nobody can give you the reply to this question but each one of us must look for the answer and, once its found, it will be the eternal truth about man!

Teaching Objective

Self analysis, search for knowing, development of intuition, correct identification.

Personality Test

- What in your opinion made Andha see without his eyes?
- Do you think it is necessary for all of us to see through our inner eyes? Why?
- Do you judge through your intelligence whenever you see or read some thing?
- When somebody you know is dead, what do you weep for? His body or something that has gone out of his body?
- What has left his body?

Questions

a. Can you describe your dream that you had seen yesterday?
b. How do you think you saw the dream though your eyes were closed?
c. Are the eyes sufficient for seeing?
d. What allows the eyes to see?
e. When you say "my eyes" or "my body" are you the body or the owner of the body?
f. Are you good or bad, polite or rude according to your judgment?
g. What is your personality according to other people?

Carry out this Exercise

Try to convince somebody that you cannot be the body, which dies.

The half is more than the whole.
This is the TRUTH. 1.7

Teaching Value

It was a Monday morning and Maharishi Viswamitra was having a bath in the river Yamuna. The sun was on the verge of rising up in the eastern horizon.

An eagle had just captured a young mouse. You know it's almost impossible to get out of the powerful claws of an eagle. But the mouse was lucky. He escaped when the eagle was flying past the Maharishi!

Half dead, it crashed straight into the folded palms of Viswamitra while he was doing a Surya Namaskar- offering prayer to the sun. The compassionate sage cured the mouse instantly with his yogic powers. Then he took it to his home.

Although cured physically, the mouse was depressed. Pessimism had overpowered him, “What's the use of such a life?” he told him gloomily, “Always I have to run for my life from the prey birds. Look at that eagle, flying up in the sky carefree. Alas! If I were an eagle, I would have been the happiest being on earth!”

"So be it!" Smiled Rishi Viswamitra; and in a moment the mouse turned into an eagle.

He kept on flying till fatigue overcame his enthusiasm, and then set down on the topmost branch of a huge banyan tree.

What he sees! The tree's been home to so many of them and numerous other birds! Now again he felt gloomy, "look at this tree. How powerful is it. I am only a small bird. Alas! I would have been happier as a tree."

Viswamitra knew about his pessimism, so kept track of him with his extraordinary powers. So he turned him into a banyan tree!

Turned into a tree he felt happy again, "look! How powerful I am! So many birds and animals take rest under my shade. People worship me!" he kept on looking around himself happily. And what he sees! A small goat has been munching away leafs from his lower branch!

"Hay! What are you doing? Leave my leaves alone!" cried the tree. But neither the goat was able to hear him nor he could move his branch away. Now again he was gloomy, "Look at the goat! How powerful is it! I could have asked the sage to become a goat instead!" he thought sorrowfully.

In an instant the tree turned into a young goat! Happy again, he ate as much leaves as possible and jumped and played on the stones. Then he ran around quite amazed at his active body.

But a tiger had waited for a kill in the nearby bush. When he saw this young and healthy goat, his mouth watered and his tail straightened. With a big roar it jumped at him. And the goat ran for his life while cursing himself for not becoming a tiger.

Maharishi Viswamitra had been keeping a track. He instantly turned him into a big tiger! The tiger that followed him was shocked at the sight; and ran away for his life instead. And he was quite happy and proud! "Nobody can mess up with me now!" he told himself sitting on a rock.

But that also was short lived. It was a rainy season, and the cloud started raining heavily soon after. And that made the tiger gloomy again, "Oh, what is this! I'm wet and cramped. With all my powers also I can't stop this rain." He looked at the cloud sorrowfully, "Alas! How happy the cloud must be! It is moving without any restriction and flooding any place it wants! And look at me; I am so powerless and a victim at its hand!"

And he turned into a cloud! Now happy again, it rained wherever it wanted and enjoyed noticing people and animals running away to avoid him.

But high wind started blowing just then and crashed it hard against a big mountain! Most of it melted away and rained over the immobile mountain. Now very small and powerless, it was depressed again. He silently prayed, "Maharishi, I am so powerless against this Mountain! How can I live like this? Could you please make me happy again?"

In an instant there stood this majestic mountain! Nothing could shake him any more! Now he felt so powerful and proud! And standing high, he could see things above the clouds.

A strange thing happened while it was watching happily a cloud crashing against him! A small mouse had started digging a hole under its feet! The mountain's happiness was gone. Gloomy again he wondered, "Just a small mouse, and how powerful is he to make a hole inside me! And how can I be happy now?"

The all-watching Maharishi made him into a mouse again! "This is all very wonderful!" cried the mouse, immensely satisfied and happy to become a mouse. Now he felt so powerful!

Some days past when an eagle was chasing him he rushed into the hole dug inside a mountain. "Look! How powerful am I! And the eagle so powerless!!"

Therefore the same thing can be understood differently, all depends on your Perception. So why complain against what has been given to us? Isn't it wise to be content with that?

Everything depends on our internal emotional state, and for that matter our future life!

Teaching Objectives

Self analysis, self identification, relativity of phenomenon.

Personality Test

- Who is an optimist?
- Who is a pessimist?
- How did the transformations help the mouse to become an optimist?

- How would you react in front of a similar situation?
- Are your friends optimists?

Questions

a. What did you learn from the story?
b. Is there anything or anybody around you whom you think truly powerful and nobody can defeat him?
c. Did you ever feel that others have got more than what you have? Why?
d. Do you think you have got more than others? Why?
e. Do you think they also feel the same way?

Carry out this Exercise

If you feel any of your friends is pessimist how do you help him?

The world is a great laboratory in which all transformations take place. This is TRUTH 1.8

Teaching Value

Sometimes we think that the things that frighten or disturb us are useless. Is this a right method of reasoning according to you?

Take the case of a poisonous snake. It's deadly and frightful. Most people kill them because they seem useless to them. But consider this with its poison we have made life saving drugs!

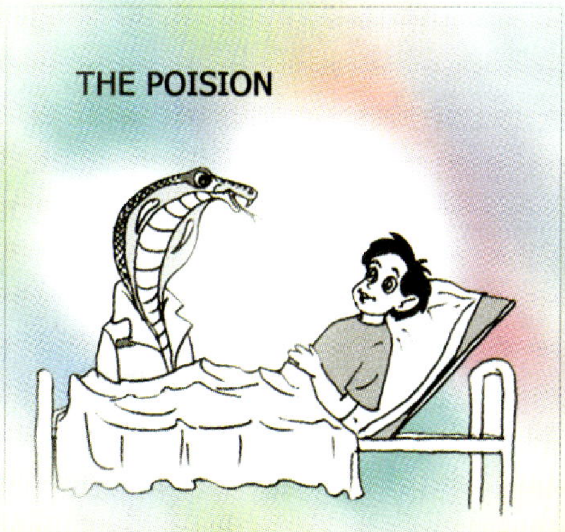

Whoever destroys nature mindlessly ignores one fundamental truth: respect for everything that exists. It is not the case of imagining what the world would be like if we could eliminate all the things we don't like or that seem to us "useless" but to accept them seeking to get the best out of them.

The ultimate fact is that the entire nature is giving, giving, giving. Nature never keeps anything. Every tree, every plant is giving. Every season is giving. At every moment Nature is giving us an opportunity to grow, to learn. Life is possible thanks to that.

The human values help us to develop this type of vision and to understand that everything has its reason for existing.

Once upon a time there was a man who was arrogant and full of himself and who passed his time criticising nature and its laws. One day, during one of his trips to a village, he stopped to rest under a banyan tree. In front of him there lay a field of watermelons.

Looking at them he exclaimed: "How absurd nature is! An insignificant plant like the watermelon plant and look how big fruits it produces, while this banyan tree is capable of producing only tiny seeds. Decidedly nature has no logic!"

He went off to sleep and woke up after several hours and found himself covered with hundreds of little seeds that had fallen from the tree. Red with shame he understood his insolence and thanked Nature. That day he realized that Nature is intelligent enough not to endow the tree with fruit proportional to its size otherwise only one of those would have been enough to kill him.

There is another important thing we must understand: when we observe nature we often note that ill turns into good. Take the example of poison. We know it has been turned into good. Would it, however, be intelligent to seek the evil because anyhow it turns into good?

Evidently not! I certainly won't go and get myself bitten by the snake to be able to experiment that it is possible to save myself from his bite by being good.

That underlines, when certain inevitable facts occur, outside our own wish and which can be considered as poisonous, there always exists a profound method of facing up to them by drawing upon the inexhaustible spring of values which live in us.

Thus we will see that the poison is not an ill but is useful. Who has not discovered that it is only from the great sorrows that arise real comprehension, tolerance, humility, respect and many other values?

Teaching Objective

Observation of nature, interconnection, good and evil, interdependence in nature, respect for the natural laws.

Personality Test

- Have you ever seen or come in contact with a snake?
- What was your reaction?
- Is it possible to love a snake?
- Have you ever thought that a snake might possess qualities? List some of these.
- What frightens you about snake?
  1. His poison.
  2. His slimy appearance.
  3. His way of moving along the ground.
- Are negative points also in you?
- How do you try to transform them and turn them into positive advantages?
- Do you know how to react to pain or sorrow?
- Do you think that with self-discipline you can train yourself to overcome the negative aspects of pain or sorrow?

Questions

a. What can the serpent's poison be used for?
b. How futile will it be if the fruits of banyan tree become the size of watermelon?
C. Why does scientists study nature?
d. What is the fundamental nature of the nature?
e. Is there something useless in the world?
f. Does there exist in the world something completely negative?

Carry out this Exercise

Invent a little story in which the hero is the snake?

Look at good thing and you'll become good. This is the path towards perfection. This is the TRUTH 1.9

Teaching Value

There is an old saying: 'the world is only the size of each man's head'. How true! Everything depends on the state of mind, which experiences differing attitude.

My uncle travels a lot, and whenever he's home he tells me many of his travel experiences.

Last time while he was traveling from Hyderabad to Delhi. Mr. Srinivas, a smalltime entrepreneur from the nearby town was also going to Delhi. They were in the same coach with another five people.

It was quite amusing to see Mr. Srinivas being extra cautious over his luggage a suitcase. The moment he entered the coach he took out two chains from his pocket and tied the suitcase below his seat. Then he double-checked the locks. Still not satisfied, he kept on looking at the co-passengers with suspicion.

My uncle is an easygoing person. When he tried to talk to him casually, he avoided and looked at him with as if he would take away his suitcase.

Anyway, my uncle had a nice time with the rest of the co-passengers as he always has. While they chatted about mundane things: each other's family, about places and other things and entertained themselves by the beverages served in the train, Mr. Srinivas remained aloof and cautious throughout the day.

At 11 o'clock in the night when he could no longer stay awake; he went to sleep although keeping a hand on the suitcase. Early morning, at around 5 o'clock my uncle woke up hearing somebody's cry. In front of him was distressed Mr. Srinivas crying like a child. The two chains were in his hand but the suitcase was gone! My uncle accompanied him to the to the railway police, where he registered an F.I.R.

Any guess how valuable his luggage was? From his descriptions the police estimated the cost about 1500 rupees, out of which the suitcase only was of seven hundred! His money, which he had kept in his pocket, was safe.

Have I told you that my uncle is a jeweller and on a business trip he carries valuables worth lakhs! He was quite relieved that his suitcase, lying just next to the stolen luggage, was untouched!

Okay, we may consider it was my uncle's good luck and Mr. Srinivas's bad luck. But was that all? Let's examine the things closely:

My uncle considered his co passengers just like his own people whereas Mr. Srinivas thought them as thieves. That is why he remained extra cautious while these people entertaining themselves. Unfortunately this very attitude might have caught the attention of the thief!

In the last fifteen years of his travel, my uncle has been robbed twice! But that has not changed his attitude of love and faith in people. He has always recovered the loss with little extra work and effort. Quite interestingly this has increased his returns! Moreover, once when he was robbed, a good man landed him his travel expenses, and since then both of them are very good friends.

When, in my heart, only love exists I will try to see in others their good qualities and will pardon their defects but if, on the other hand, exists spitefulness I will see in others only their defects and will not be able to see, as a consequence, their virtues.

Just like if I were to put on red glasses I would see every thing coloured red, if I were to put on dark glasses I would see every thing dark, if I were to put on clear glasses I would see every thing clear.

Every thing depends on the colour of the glasses. The spectacles are my way of seeing: if I put on the glasses I would see the good qualities of the things around me and if I put on the glasses of spitefulness I would see their defects.

Teaching Objective

Interior and exterior vision, self-analysis.

Personality Test

- Your mood is not dependent on your mode of seeing? Why?
- When you have spiteful thoughts are you in a good mood or not? Why?
- When you have good thoughts do you always smile? Why?
- How much time do you think passes between one thought and the next?
- Does your actions depend on the type of mood you are in? Why?
- By carrying out good actions can you have an influence on your mood? Why?
- When you have carried out your duty to the full do you feel happy?

Questions

a. What was the colour of Mr. Srinivas's glasses?
b. What was the colour of the glasses of my uncle?
c. If you put clear glasses how do you see around you?
d. If you put on either the coloured glasses or dark glasses how do you see?
e. What do these glasses represent?

Carry out this Exercise

Describe an incident you have experienced; and your mood swing after that.

Time is Life. Time lost is life lost.
This is the TRUTH 1.10

Teaching Value

...And he started running. "Is there anybody in this jungle who can run faster than me?" he mumbled himself while running and jumping in a jolly mood. He made a big leap to see where his foolish competitor has reached. But no one is following. He smiled to himself, "perhaps he will take a whole year to reach the finishing line."

In the next turning there is the finishing line. He could see the bigger animals gathered for celebration of his victory. The cheer leaders the crow, the toad, the peacock and the elephant are cheering as loud as they can cheer. "But wait, what are they cheering at? I have not yet reached", thought the rabbit. He hurried his footsteps.

When he reached the finishing line nobody cheered for him. He looked at the rabbits gathered there, they were all ashamed.

At a distance he saw the proud tortoise on a stone. Every body has gathered around him and were praising him. The elder rabbit scoffed at him, "how could you lose to a tortoise; you rascal? The world will never forget that a rabbit lost to a tortoise in a race!" And all the rabbits disappeared into the jungle leaving him alone.

Oh yes! I am only telling you the famous race of the rabbit and the tortoise, where you knew what happened. It's simply that the rabbit could not understand he had slept for such a long time.

Tell me when we wake up in the morning how many hours do we think we have slept? Not certainly the eight hours of the clock, but much less!

Why? Because at a certain point the mind cancels out, and time is not perceived, and the world vanishes for us.

Now consider this. What might the tortoise be thinking while crossing the sleeping rabbit? For him time expanded almost until infinity. How desperately he desired time to be a bit fast!

The passing of time is connected with moods, and relationship with others and surrounding world.

What instruments do we know which measure time? The clock, the hourglass, the sundial (the world's biggest sundial is Jantar Mantar, New Delhi), the sun, the moon, the stars, etc.

These measure time with great precision. But, as we have seen, there exists another instrument capable of measuring it and that is the human mind. But it is not precise like the others: it lies to us and does not tell the truth. Time passes fast when I am enjoying myself and passes slowly when I am sad. Why do we say that the Sunday passes quickly and Monday never passes? Doesn't a day last 24 hours for everyone?

Can we then say that the world is a mental phenomenon?

We **exist** beyond the world and our own mind; we **experience** the world through our mind!

The truth about us is that all our mental experience of joy and suffering does not touch our true reality, which is beyond all this.

Teaching Objective

Reality and self analysis.

Personality Test

- If you sleep 8 hours during the night, how many hours do you feel that you have slept when you wake up in the morning?
- Why does time "stops" for you sometimes?
- Would it be possible for you to perceive the world that surrounds you without time? Why?
- Does passing time give you pleasure or make you afraid?
- Is time measurable only with the clock?

Questions

a. Why did the rabbit lose the race?
b. In reality who is faster - tortoise or rabbit?
c. With how many instruments can you measure time?
d. Why does Sunday, in general, pass quickly whereas Monday seems a longer day?
e. When mind measures the time does it err or does it tell the truth?
f. If time were all of a sudden to stop what would happen?
g. What is time?

Carry out this Exercise

On what occasions have you wished that time would stop?

The truth will always come to the surface. This is the TRUTH 1.11

Teaching Value

The power of truth reveals itself with time and, in the end, we realize that it is much better to tell the truth, behave well and not do ill to anybody because sooner or later, as an old proverb says, "the truth always comes to the surface."

I am sure you already know many stories where truth triumphs. How about this one the story of the frog and the cuckoo?

Well, it's a folk tale from Bhutan. Long ago there lived a big, fat frog who was married to a cuckoo. They lived inside a dense forest in the foothills of the great Himalayas.

The cuckoo loved and cared for the frog very much. Every day at the daybreak she got up before any one else, went searching for food far off into the jungle; by any means found some delicious juicy insects and brought those back to the frog. By the time the frog got up from the bed breakfast was ready besides him. After devouring the breakfast he would go out to have sunbath in the open and chatter with the jungle folks passingby.

While the cuckoo did all the cleaning and washing the frog kept on looking at other's beautiful wives and cursed himself for marrying a wife that was jet black. "Look at fox's wife. Oh! How pretty is she, her chicks are like rose, skin is rich and her tail is as beautiful as a golden duster. How lucky is that slow wit fox!" shied the frog, "look at my wife; as if coming out of a coal mine. Alas! What an ill luck of mine!"

But when cuckoo was near he talked very sweetly to her and praised her, told her how much he loved her and how he wanted to die for her.

Poor innocent cuckoo believed him so much. She felt herself so lucky that she had a loving husband. And she tried to bring more rare and delicious insects to the frog as gifts of love. So time passed like this.

Then one day the eagle informed the cuckoo that her mother was ill. She stayed in Tibet, on the north of the great snow clad peaks. Cuckoo decided to go. The frog was very happy inside, but kept on telling her how he loved her and how he'll miss her. Early next day, after bringing breakfast for the frog she flew over to the distant mountains.

Now alone, the frog was in a merrymaking mood. His stomach full, he stretched out his limbs in all directions and gave a loud yawn and set under the morning sun singing happily. Slowly the jungle folks surrounded him listening to his funny songs. He sang all the derogatory words meant for cuckoo and the animals around him laughed heartily at that.

While the show continued the cuckoo returned halfway because she had forgotten the medicine for her mother. She saw the gathering, and heard the frog singing. She set on a tree branch hidden from him and listened all the rubbish against her. Poor cuckoo shook her head in shame and humiliation as her eyes were filled with tears. So, this is what he thought of her! Suddenly she flew out from her hiding place and confronted him, quivering with emotion.

"It's not been a whole day since we parted and this is how you disgrace me! From now on I shall have nothing to do with you." The frog was taken aback by surprise and lay there staring at her with his bulging eyes that bulged even further. He was so ashamed of himself that he leapt into the nearby pond with a big splash and never came out again.

"The water has been defiled with your lowly presence. I shall not drink it even if I have to die of thirst," told the cuckoo loud before flying away.

Since that day, people of Bhutan believe, cuckoo does not drink from ponds; it drinks early dewdrops on the grass and leaves.

This beautiful story tells us time is an infallible revealer of the truth even though we sometimes think "can get away with it!" He who has the profound conviction of the existence of imminent justice and that the truth always comes to the surface, will be better able to endure apparent injustices. In fact no one can get away with it because, as we always reap what we sow and this is what we call imminent justice.

Teaching Objective

Interior honesty, seeking for the truth, the value of time

Personality Test

- Do you always repeat the same error even if you know it?
- What do you think of a person who tells lies?
- How would you behave in this regard?
- What is, according to you, the result of a lie?
- Do you think that sometimes it is possible to tell lies?
- Someone who always tell lies, is he guilty or ill?
- Do you think that it is possible to be cured from the bad habit of always telling lies?

Questions

a. Why the frog did not love the cuckoo?
b. Why the cuckoo believed her husband loved her very much?
c. What happened when the cuckoo was absent?
d. Is it possible to hide something?
e. Do you believe in the profound thought "we always reap what we sow"?

Carry out this Exercise

Think of a past experience of yours where the truth ultimately came into the surface.

The
Right Action

The right idea put into practice is a just action. This is the RIGHT ACTION 2.1

Teaching Value

Life always imposes decisions and we must learn to make them correctly. By thorough examination of the preceding value, the Truth, we have learned the principles on which our life is based and what are the instruments at our disposal to enable us to experience it.

The value titled the Right Action hence refers to the practical application of the principles of truth. We have, furthermore, learned that the two instruments which accompany us all along the way are the mind and the heart.

Do you know who Yudhisthir was? Yes, you are right! He was the eldest Pandava, widely respected for his wisdom and truthfulness.

It was the first day of Kauravas and Pandavas in school. Guru Dronacharya welcomed all his little pupils and gave the first lesson of their life:

"Satyam Vada, Dharma-chara", which means ALWAYS TELL THE TRUTH AND DO WHAT IS RIGHT. Dronacharya explained the meaning of these two lines elaborately and asked them to memorise.

Early next morning when the class started Guruji asked previous day's lesson. And all of them recited the two lines. But Yudhisthira could not recite.

Next day again Guruji asked Yudhisthira about his first lesson, but he was unable to reply.

Four days passed in this manner.

Finally Guru Dronacharya lost his patience and demanded an explanation in front of the whole class.

Yudhisthira stood up with eyes upon his feet and replied slowly, "Guruji, I am trying hard to implement those two lines in my day to day life. Still I can't resist telling one or two lies in a day.

It would of course be a lie if I tell you that I have memorized the lesson as I have not yet put it into practice. Therefore I could not recite the two lines.

Acharya Dronacharya and rest of the pupils were spellbound!

It was the same Yudhisthira who grew up to become 'Dharma Raaj'; and lead the fight against 'Adharma' in Mahabharata. It was Yudhisthira who listened to his heart or conscience. The rest of the students had listened to their minds only which had memorized the lesson.

The conscience is hence our policeman which tells us whenever we do any wrong. But do we always listen to our conscience?

Let's take a look at the three pictures:

The child in the first image looks at the banana skin lying on the road but passes on without doing anything. It doesn't interest him as to whether the banana skin could be dangerous for himself or others.

Does this mean that he does not have a conscience? No! It only means that he is using the mind which says to him, "When you yourself have avoided it that is sufficient! What do you care about the others?" he is completely deaf to the voice of his conscience.

The second child knows that it is dangerous but he doesn't want to 'dirty his hands' and says to himself "there are garbage collectors who are paid for this!", then calls someone else to pick it up. How many people are there who delegate to others their own duties!

Finally the third child is he who carries out the just action, following the dictates of his conscience. To the question; "which child performs the right action?" the automatic reply comes, "The one that is smiling".

In fact he is smiling with satisfaction, the one who had carried out his duty up to the end.

Teaching Objective

Interior maturity and character, love and respect for others, civic sense.

Personality Test

- What do you like most in Yudhisthira?
- Do you think you apply the principles of truth and right action in your life?
- What do you think about the banana skin incident?

- Have you ever found yourself in such a situation?
- How did you behave?
- Find a synonym for laziness, indifference, selfishness.
- Why has the last child a happy look on his face?

Questions

a. Do you know any other story from Mahabharata?
b. What did Yudhisthira become after he grew up?
c. Is a banana skin on the ground dangerous? Why?
d. Which is the right action: that in the first, the second or the third image?
e. Why are the others not right?
f. If we know that a thing is right why don't we do it?

Carry out this Exercise

Give a practical example of a right action and, from today on, name a resolution.

Facing up the negatives with the positive energy within us can transform them. This is the RIGHT ACTION 2.2

Teaching Value

In the presence of hate, jealousy and anger we retreat, get frightened, and we surrender, letting these energies overpower us.

But the right way of acting in these cases is to face up to them with the positive energies within us.

Have you heard about the Brahmin and his wife's story?

Well, many years ago in a small village in Andhra Pradesh lived a poor and benevolent Brahmin. He was such a sweetheart that he could not refuse anybody anything. The shrewd people in the village took advantage of him all the time

During the lunch hours one of the crooks would just come to him and act out as if he's hungry for two days. Poor Brahmin could not refuse and invite him for lunch.
His wife had to keep deliberate fast. Sometimes even their children had to remain hungry because of these untimely guests. After many quarrels also she could not prevent this benevolent Brahmin from inviting the crooks.

One day she realized that anger wouldn't solve her problem. Therefore she concentrated on her positive energies and thought out a plan to get rid of the thugs.

That day also a thug accompanied her husband home during lunch hours. Instead of getting angry she invited him with a bright smile. The Brahmin was happy not to hear any harsh words.

He requested his guest to take a seat in the drawing room and went to have a bath to the nearby pond.

In the mean time his wife cleaned a corner of the drawing room, and planted a huge club against the wall. The club was generally used those days to grind grains. She then put flowers around it and started worshipping.

The guest, alarmed at the sight, asked what was she doing.

"Don't you know", she replied, "it is our custom. Whenever any guest comes home for lunch, the head of the house gives him a blow with this ancestral 'club god'. Now that my father-in-law is no more, my husband would carry out this ritual".

The guest started to elope. Wife requested him, "please don't go. It will not be very painful; just that you may lose your consciousness for a while."

Even more alarmed, the guest walked away with quick steps. Just then the Brahmin returned and surprised at the sight. He went inside angrily and asked his wife what had happened.

"My dear, your guest asked for this club as 'Dakhshina'. This is the only club I have. If he will take away how would I grind the grains? I refused and see how he is walking away with anger" replied his wife innocently.

"Nonsense lady, how could you refuse such a mundane thing to our guest?" The Brahmin was angry, "give it to me. Better I should hurry up and give it to him". He ran after the guest carrying the club. When the thug looked back and saw the Brahmin running after him with that vicious club, he ran even faster and disappeared within no time. Life after all is more precious than a free meal!

Brahmin laughed heartily when he got to know the truth. Although he scolded her for her lies, he also appreciated her intelligence as he could get rid of the thug.

Rumors spread fast! From then on nobody would ask him for a free meal!

We can notice three aspects among the three characters:

The Brahmin is simple and god fearing. In this case fear overpowered his conscience! Even knowing that he is being fooled he still invited so that god would not be angry with him. As a result, though, his children and wife stayed hungry!

The second character, his intelligent wife understood her negative energy anger; and consciously fought it to get an amicable plan. In this case she transformed her energy and used it positively. She got the result without insulting his husband or the thug.

In the third case, the thug, who had no fear of God and wrath of a Brahmin, had the fear of getting thrashed up. This negative energy caused him to run away without even understanding the situation!

The just action consists in fighting our negative tendencies to the last and not allowing ourselves ever to get discouraged, conscious of the fact that, in the end, good will always triumph.

Personality Test

- When you get angry, are you capable of calming your anger or do you let yourself get involved by the "enemy"?
- Similarly when you get scared what do you do?
- Are you capable of gathering together, in the moment, all your positive qualities of courage, faith, humility, peace and will?
- What is indispensable for winning the fight?
- Do you recognise the negative energies within you?

Questions

a. Do you know anybody like the Brahmin in the story?
b. have you ever invited anybody to your home for lunch?
c. How do you treat your guests?
d. How do you define the character of the Brahmin's wife?
e. Have you ever tried to fight with your negative qualities?

Carry out this Exercise

Tell about a struggle between good and evil which has taken place inside yourself and from which you emerged victorious?

Man must "operate" in the hands of his conscience. This is the RIGHT ACTION 2.3

Teaching Value

Man, in order to pass his life usefully to himself and to others, must learn three important things: Discipline, Duty and Respect for others.

Our mother or father gives us an order to which it is our duty to obey instead of evaluating it and questioning it.

Once upon a time in an ashram of a renowned teacher there were fifty disciples. One day the teacher thought of testing his pupils. He called up all of them early morning.

"Boys, today is an auspicious day. So let's take a break from the studies and clean up the ashram well." He told them, "Why don't you go get the bamboo baskets first?"

There were many baskets and containers made of bamboo lying in the ashram. Every body could obtain one for themselves.

When they gathered again with the bamboo baskets, Guruji ordered them, "Hurry up! Go to the river and bring water in the baskets. We will wash the floors before painting it with fresh cow dung.

The disciples were surprised. "Guruji, how can we bring the water with these baskets that have so many of holes; and the river is too far. All the water will flow down within a few steps!"

The teacher did not even listen to them, "go and don't waste my time. Do as I said"

All the pupils went to the river, but there was chaos and confusion among them. "How is it possible?" some would say, "however, we have got a day long break. Let's play and swim."

Some of them tried once or twice. The water would flow down from the basket within ten fifteen steps. They were skeptical of his intentions, "Guruji, perhaps, has gone mad or harassing all of us!" They kept the baskets at the river bank and started playing.

Then there were others who went to the village to find some earthen pitchers, against Guruji's orders.

But only one of them was doing exactly what he was asked to do. He would fill the basket up with water and start towards ashram. When the water flowed down, he would come back and fill up again. Numerous times he was unsuccessful. Yet he did not give up and tried throughout the day.

Many of his friends laughed and passed remarks, but nothing distracted him.

Finally, by the evening he reached the ashram with basket full of water!

You know the dried wood or bamboo fattens when kept inside the water for long. That is why the holes in the basket had filled up by the evening! Now the basket was as watertight as an earthen pitcher.

All his companions had returned back empty handed few hours back. And everybody was waiting for him.

Now they were surprised and cheered him.

Guruji declared him his best disciple and gave them the lesson of the day, "Nothing is impossible. Only what we need is patience and determination."

"Never question those who are your well wishers. Just do as they say"

Teaching Objective

Social conscience, interdependence, value of discipline and devotion.

Personality Test

- Give a definition of discipline.
- What is the sense of duty?
- What does respect for others mean?
- Does duty exist without discipline?
- Does respect exist without duty?
- Have you done your duty if you have studied at home but are wild and undisciplined in class or the other way round?
- Have you done your duty when you get good marks at school but do not respect your parents at home?

Questions

a. How many kinds of disciples are there?
b. Do you follow the order of your parents and teachers? To what extent?
c. Had you been given the same task what would you do?
d. Have you remembered any occasion when you did not obey your parent's orders?
e. Do you feel you were right by not obeying them?
f. Can there be love without respect or respect without love?

Carry out this Exercise

Demonstrate the statement that discipline, duty and respect for others if taken separately have no meaning.

Criticise only if you prove that you can do it better. This is the RIGHT ACTION 2.4

Teaching Value

Criticism is to blame and disapprove.

Generally we criticise people with words because this is the easiest way and does not require any effort. Behind the criticism, in this case, there lies a feeling of jealousy or envy or, perhaps, only sterile habit.

Of course we know about the Damocles' sword! Don't we?

Damocles was one of the royal bards of king Damascus. His job was to flatter the king in his court. Of course he did his job well. No one flattered the king like Damocles. He, therefore, became famous in the city.

As a result he himself gathered some sycophants around him. They would follow him wherever he went and kept on flattering him.

Slowly he started believing that the king's job is quite easy. It is he who has made the king a king. Otherwise he would be just nobody.

"Oh! Come on; what is there in being a king? Any body can become one. You get to wear lavish dresses eat and drink costliest things and pass time among beautiful dancers. What else a king does? Ha..ha..ha." He would remark to his nodding admirers.

When the city rumored about Damocles, the king got to know it. He loved him, therefore wanted to give him an eye opening lesson. Next day he called upon Damocles in the middle of the court.

"What are we hearing Damocles? You are criticising us among the ordinary people! Do you understand you are destroying my reputation among our subjects?"

Damocles' ego was hurt, "My lord, I.. I only said you entertain yourself with dancers, lavish food and drink. And you don't have to worry a bit!"

"And you said any body can become a king?"

"Y..y.. yes! But isn't it true my lord?"

"Is it? Why don't you try it out for yourself?"

And so it was declared in the kingdom that Damocles would be the king the next day.

The whole night he could not sleep with excitement. All kinds of royal food and drinks appeared in his dreams. There would be beautiful women around him. It would be so much fun to sit on the throne! And the king would flatter him! What else does he need?!

The king kept his words next day. Every body saluted Damocles when he occupied the throne and the king sang the songs of flattery. Everything was so exciting!

Suddenly his eyes fall on a very sharp and heavy sword hovering exactly over his head. ..And it was tied with a single strand of horse hair!!

His heart almost came to his mouth. "W..w..why is this sword over my head?" he pleaded to the king.

"It is the custom. You keep your mind out of that my lord," Smiled the king, "Look, how the people are greeting you and the women admiring you!"

The sword trill a bit when a blow of wind hit it.

Damocles was full of perspiration, "Please spare me my lord. At this moment I am prepared to leave the throne."

"Sorry my lord", the king smiled again; "you have to sit there till the sun is set. It's the custom."

Damocles, perhaps, died a thousand deaths on a single day! As soon as the Sun set, he jumped out of the throne for safety and fell on the feet of Damascus, "My lord, I beg pardon a million times; and never ever I'll criticise you in this life!"

Both were happy to be back in their previous roles.

THE SIGN OF REAL HUMANITY IS CONSISTENCY BETWEEN WORDS AND ACTION. PRACTICE WHAT YOU PREACH. CRITICISM IS A PROCESS WHICH, TO BE CONSTRUCTIVE, MUST INVOLVE FIRST OF ALL OURSELVES AND OUR CAPACITY TO REPEAT THE OPERATION WITHOUT ERROR AND BETTER.

Teaching Objective

Use of the critical faculty, strength of will, use of latent talent, formation of character.

Personality Test

- When someone criticises you how do you react?
    1. Criticise in your turn?
    2. Do you remain indifferent?
    3. Do you get angry?
- According to you has criticism become, today, a common habit? Give examples.
- Could time and energy used in criticism be put to a better use?
- Would you be able to criticise without offending anyone?
- How are you going to criticise somebody's work?

Questions

a. Do you also think a king, in today's case, a minister spend his time lavishly?
b. Do you think Damocles was right when he criticized Damascus?

c. Why was he quick to retire from the throne?
d. What does criticism mean?
e. How many types of criticism are there?
f. What type is that which corresponds to the right action?
g. What is silent criticism?

Carry out this Exercise

How do you make a long line short without touching it? Simply by drawing a longer line near it. Similarly how do you criticise somebody's work? Explain it to your friends.

That which I have spent was mine, that which I have kept I have lost.
This is the RIGHT ACTION 2.5

Teaching Value

Here is a folk tale from Bihar the tale of 'Ekki' and 'Dukki'.

Ekki and Dukki were two sisters; lived in a small village in Bihar with their parents. Do you know why their names were so? That's because Ekki had only a single strand of hair over her head while Dukki had two strands.

Dukki was of course very proud of her hair, "don't you see I have two strands of beautiful hair! Look at Ekki, only a single hair..so ugly!" Ekki did not care about her sister's demeaning comparisons and played happily with her friends the street dogs, pigeons, sparrows and all the children of their neighbourhood.

Once when mom asked Dukki to collect firewood from the jungle she refused straightaway, "mom, don't you see I am busy combing my hair. Why don't you ask Ekki?"

Ekki agreed readily and started for jungle. Mom had given her puffed rice in case she felt hungry.

On her way she saw a cow tied to a bush full of thorns, mingleed around it and is crying in pain. She released her by cutting the rope. She thanked her and went away searching for her hungry calf. And Ekki concentrated in collecting firewood.

Deep inside the jungle, she suddenly saw a horrible looking old woman lying under a tree. When she came nearer the old woman asked for food and a little water.

Ekki gave her all her puffed rice to eat and brought water from the nearby stream.

The old woman felt well and told her, "Poor child, I ate all your stuff. Now you are hungry. Go to a little farther to your right, and you'll find a wild tree full of fruits to eat." And she went away.

Ekki stopped when she saw the tree and ate some fruits, which were delicious. Suddenly she felt something on her head. She touched it and lo! Beautiful thick hair had grown all over her head!

She was very happy and wanted to take some fruits for her sister. But all the fruits from the tree had disappeared!

On her way home it had become dark. While she was wandering how to find her route the cow came to her rescue. And she reached home delighted.

Dukki felt wretched now and quite jealous of Ekki because she had so much of beautiful hair now and look at her, she had only two strands of hair!

Next day she started for the jungle carrying 'Halwa-puri'. On the way she found the cow tied to the bush as Ekki had told. But she was scared that the thorns would prick her, and went away without releasing the cow.

The old woman was there as Ekki had mentioned. She told her, "Budhia, I have brought halwa-puri for you because I want better hair than Ekki's. And she gave only one puri and a little halwa.

The old woman smiled and asked her to bring some water. But Dukki refused straightaway, "The stream is too far. You go yourself. Now just let me know where the tree is."

The old woman smiled again and pointed towards the tree and went away.

Dukki ate some fruits and waited and waited for the hair to come up. But nothing happened. She rushed after the old women angrily but could not find her anywhere. By that time it was dark and she could not find her way back. And nobody came to her rescue.

Somehow she reached home next morning. She had not a single hair now and the thorns had pinched all over her body.

Never again she compared herself with Ekki!

Now let's try to understand why Ekki had so many friends although she had only one hair. It's because she knew the art of giving, she shared things with them; whereas Dukki always thought of only receiving. She wanted everybody to treat her better than Ekki.

That is why Ekki was happy all the time while Dukki pained herself by comparing and feeling proud that she had more.

Receiving gives a limited amount of joy whereas GIVING GIVES US A JOY WHICH IS WITHOUT END AND WHICH RENEWS ITSELF.

Lets take a small example mummy had filled your lunchbox with something delicious. And you eat it alone, sharing with nobody. While returning home you look at a boy eating chocolate and your mouth watered. Look! You have already forgotten the happiness of the lunchtime. Now you want more happiness!

Suppose you share with your friends, they praise your mummy and you feel very happy. You tell your mummy how your friends praised her. She feels happy. In return you feel happy again.

Next day during lunchtime your friends remember yesterday's food and you feel happy yet again and so on and so forth!

You see, how wonderful experience is giving; and TRUE HAPPINESS CONSISTS IN GIVING AND NOT IN RECEIVING!

Teaching Objective

Altruism, self-analysis, imagination at the service of noble sentiments.

Personality Test

- Are you happier when you give a present or receive one?
- Why are you happy?
- Are you glad to give a present to someone you don't like?
- Does it tire you more to give or to receive?
- Make a list of the names of those you know who have always given without ever asking anything.

Questions

a. Why Ekki had more friends than Dukki?
b. What would you do if you were in place of Dukki?
c. Do you always need money to give a gift?
d. Is telling your mummy how your friends had praised her is a gift to your mummy?
e. What does your happiness depend upon: yourself or others?

Carry out this Exercise

In a year how many occasions are there for receiving or giving a gift? List them.

Tell me how you choose and I will tell you who you are. This is the RIGHT ACTION 2.6

Teaching Value

The plants choose only 26 elements for their use leaving aside the other 79 existing in the earth!

Do we ourselves know how to choose in the same way the food for our senses and our mind so that it assists in our development and does not damage it?

We know what food is good for our stomach. If we take something bad, we end up having stomach problems. Similarly what is the most suitable food for our tongue..other than tasting? Of course they are soft words, friendly and comforting, and also interesting and elevated conversation, etc.

What is the suitable food for our ears? Listening to elevating conversation and good councils and good music. What food is good for our eyes? Reading good books, magazines, newspapers and watching good shows.

The deer was young and energetic. He had a beautiful body and long horns. When the jackal saw him instantly he wanted to have its meat. "I can't kill this strong deer.

Let me think of some plan", he told to himself and went near the deer and wanted to be his friend, "Oh my! What beautiful eyes you have and look at your horn ..and your muscles! You are of course the strongest being on the earth".

The innocent deer was placated thoroughly and asked him who he was.

"Oh I am a poor little jackal who has no friends in this big jungle".

The deer sure was unable to choose what is good for him, "Ok! I am your friend from this moment!" and from that day they started roaming around together.

His old friend the crow tried to alert the deer, "My dear, how on earth do you befriend this jackal? His intentions don't look good to me."

The jackal heard it and was angry, "Your mind is as black as your body. Why don't you stay away from us? You see it is a shame for Sir Deer to have a friend like you who has no looks and a jarring voice."

The deer did not say a single word, for he was blind with pride. And the crow flew away feeling sorry for him.

Next day the jackal took him to a lush green corn field near the jungle, "look what beautiful vegetation! Have a fill and you don't have to go here and there in search of food!"

The deer started eating the corns but the jackal stayed out, "you see I am a non-vegetarian. Let me go and have something for myself"...he was well aware of the strong trap that the farmer had put there for invaders.

He knew that the farmer would kill the deer there and he would have a feast of sweet deer meat!

Sure enough the deer got caught in the trap!

The more he tried to escape the tighter became the knots. He cried for help. The jackal made his excuse, "oh dear! I am so sorry, but I can't cut the trap. Today is an auspicious day and I can't touch the rope made of leather!" He went hiding behind a bush and waited for the farmer to come.

Now only the deer was able to understand the intentions of the jackal, but it was too late.

Fortunately the crow was flying by. He heard the deer crying for help, and instantly came down to him. The intelligent crow understood everything. "Don't worry," he said, "when the farmer comes you act as if you are dead breathe very slow and fill your stomach with air. I will be sitting near your eye as if eating it. Just run as fast as you can the moment I give you a call."

When the farmer came and saw a dead deer, he did not tie its legs before opening the trap. As soon as he opened the trap the crow called and the deer rose up with a start and ran away.

The shocked farmer threw his stick with all his force, but it could not reach the deer. Instead it hit the jackal sitting behind the bush, leaving him with a broken leg and a blind eye!

The right action Therefore also is to choose between what to do and what not to do.

Teaching Objective

Discrimination, observation of nature.

Personality Test

- What makes you decide one food rather than another?
- What are the factors that influence you in this choice?
- How many times a day do you have to make a choice? Give an example.
- What do you understand by food for mouth?
- What do you understand by food for the ears?
- What do you understand by food for the eyes?

Questions

a. How do the plants manage to choose only 26 out of 105 elements in the earth?
b. What do you learn from the deer's act?
c. While choosing your food do you consider the source of it?
d. Why do the flowers and plants never make a mistake while choosing the right thing for themselves?
e. Why is man subject to making errors?
f. Would evolution be possible without good and evil?

Carry out this Exercise

Describe the choices you have made during a day and explain why.

Doing the right thing at the right time is the only way to reach our destination. This is the RIGHT ACTION 2.7

Teaching Value

Let me tell you a beautiful story of the ant and the grasshopper:

It was a hot summer day and the ant was very busy. He, along with his other pals, was running around for food. They all were quite exhausted in the heat of the sun; thin bodies were almost wet with perspiration. Yet all of them were engaged in searching for food, calling others for help, breaking up the food into pieces and carrying home one after another.

The grasshopper was relaxing under the shade of a big leaf cursing the sun. He had eaten enough for the day. Then he had had a nap. Feeling fresh after the nap he was now concentrating on a folk song in his shrill voice.

The ant was passing by. Grasshopper stopped him, "Ant bhai, please stop and listen to this beautiful song: Aa….aa…..".

"No dear", interrupted the ant, "I have to carry home all this food. This is just not the time to relax."

Interrupted, he felt angry, "What rubbish! You are so tiny. You need just a morsel to fill your stomach. But you have already taken home so much food that even I can eat for a week. Everyday you people carry home food all the time. Please tell me what do you do with so much of food?"

Ant's answer was simple, "saving for the rainy days."

"Oh you fool ants!" the grasshopper was bored of the answer, "Don't you see how I am enjoying my life? Life is for entertainment, you know! Look at me. When I am filled for the day, I sing, I dance, hop and play, I sleep; and I fantasize about my would-be wife. My dear ant, that's life; and not working the whole day like coolies!"

Ant smiled at him and walked away. The grasshopper just could not understand why the ant spoiled his days fearing an unforeseen future.

Then came the rainy season and there was water everywhere. He was not at all prepared.

He coaxed the cloud for raining so hard, the water for logging everywhere; but alas! He could not get a single morsel of food for seven days!

Finally, wet, sick and starved, he reached somehow at the ant's home the big anthill. And what he finds! Ant and his all the pals are having a carnival. Dry and crispy food is piled up before them. And they are enjoying the rains through their tiny windows; eating as much as they can, chatting with one another, discussing finer things of life, laughing and roaring at jokes; children playing and making merry!

Grasshopper was in tears while devouring the food given by the ant, "Ant bhai, you saved my life today. Now I understand what did you mean at that time."

Had the grasshopper acted in time he also would have saved himself from starvation.

Every moment of our life is precious. Only he can find the finer aspects of life who works sincerely and does not waste any moment in mundane things.

As in the case of the ant, the so-called enjoyments will come to you automatically. But do not get carried away by them.

Teaching Objective

Perseverance, patience, cooperation, knowledge of our own limits.

Personality Test

- In your attitude do you feel you are more like ant or the grasshopper?
- Would it be possible to modify your attitude?
- What is the difference between the enjoyment of the grasshopper and the enjoyment of the ant?
- Do you feel like working with others?

Questions

a. What would you do if you were in place of the grasshopper?
b. Who enjoyed his life more? The grasshopper or the ant?
c. Have you ever felt, just before your exams, that you could have prepared yourself a little earlier?
d. Who in your class do you consider is the grasshopper and who is the ant?
e. Who is the author of your destiny?
f. Why does the ant reach his objective?

Carry out this Exercise

Describe an incident where you or somebody you know faces the consequences of a previous action? It may be good or bad.

Intoxication Leads to a sick Mind. Avoid it. This is the RIGHT ACTION 2.8

Teaching Value

What is life without a little fun? It fills life with colours and immense pleasure. Does that mean we go to any extent for the sake of fun, certainly not!

As we have already discussed, our life depends on what we choose and how we choose.

Sukhbindar could not choose the right thing for him when he was in school. He made some bad friends and took to smoking and drinking influenced by them.

Raju played guitar well. We, the rest of the class had fun listening to him during class breaks. All of us would participate, some drumming the tables with rhythm while some singing to his tunes. In the afternoons we played games. Munna wrote poetry well. Very often we gathered to listen to his favourite 'four lines'. I tell you we had so much fun every day that I can remember all those days even after so many years.

Only Sukhbindar avoided our gatherings and slipped away to have a cigarette. Sometimes he got drunk. And he always thought these are the 'fun' things! He even tried some drugs to get a 'high'!

After school I went ahead with my career and lost contact with my school pals. Only a few months ago I met Sukhibindar on my trip to Jalandhar, his native city.

Now completely addicted, he was already looking like a ghost. His business was suffering. There were always family tensions. His wife scolded him all the time; and in return he often beat his wife. Life had become a hell for him.

He remembered the old days and cursed himself for not listening to us, and requested me if I could somehow help him get rid of his addictions.

I knew of a Maulvi saheb who helped people get rid of intoxication. So I gave him his address, wished him good luck and went ahead with my work.

Early next day he went there. Maulvi Saheb was busy with his disciples. After a long waiting, he called him, "Yes beta, tell me what do you want?"

Sukhbindar told him all his worries and requested to help him dump his bad habit anyhow.

"Ok! Come in the evening and we will see what can be done."

Sukhbinder went there in the evening, but Maulvi saheb was still busy doing some mundane things. He waited and waited. After two hours of waiting when he went near the Maulvi saheb he started to go out of his house.

He followed him, "S..S..Saheb, you had said in the morning you will help me out. So please do some thing.."
Unfazed, Maulvi saheb went straight near a tree, embraced it with his two hands and stood there.

Sukhbindar didn't know what to do! He requested him again.

"Don't you see", retorted the Maulvi, "the tree is not leaving me, otherwise I would have helped you with all my heart."

Now Sukhbindar was somewhat irritated at this funny behaviour, "Come on Sir, its not the tree! It's you who is embracing the tree!"

Maulvi Saheb smiled, "Is it? I am also seeing the same thing in you! How can intoxication embrace you? It is you who has embraced him".

Sukhbindar had got the answer!He greeted him goodbye and went home determined.

Alcohol, smoking, drugs, all that intoxicate the human body and mind are among the most dangerous menaces for our lives.

These are absolutely not fun!

Teaching Objective

Denunciations of phenomena which degrade the personality, lucidity, force of character and will.

Personality Test

- Have you ever looked at a drunken man and noted his behaviour?
- What does the word "drugs" mean to you?
- According to you what should be done to prevent the use of alcohol?
- Why does a man get drunk?
- Have you ever helped a drunk to get back home?
- Does a drunken man merit blame or compassion?

Questions

a. Why did Sukhbindar start drinking?
b. What did the others do for fun and entertainment?
c. What do you do for fun?
d. What is your favorite pastime?
   1. Music and dancing
   2. Games and sports
   3. Painting and other extra-curricular activities?
e. Why do we say that man is the product of his habits?
f. Is the publicity in newspapers and television for wine or alcohol and cigarettes damaging?
g. Do you know a friend of yours who drink alcoholic beverages? Why?

Carry out the Exercise

Carry out a research project on alcoholism in your country and explain what you would do to stop it.

Man is like a seed. Well cultivated he will yield good fruit. This is the RIGHT ACTION 2.9

Teaching Value

Life's result will be good or bad, poor or rich, according to the state of our heart. If the heart is pure and full of good sentiments we will obtain good result. The first thing to do is to eliminate from our heart the six negative sentiments that infest it like weeds in a field: JEALOUSY, GREED, SELF-CENTEREDNESS (EGOISM), HATE, ANGER AND ATTACHMENT TO POSSESSIONS.

An ascetic ('Sadhu') was on his daily tour of begging.

When he knocked a door, the lady of the house came along. He asked for alms, she in return asked for some 'Upadesha'- good advice.

The ascetic refused, "not today, tomorrow."

"Then come tomorrow for alms" snapped back the housewife.

Next day the ascetic put some dried cow dung, sand and dirt in his bagging bowl and went to the lady.

She had made delicious 'kheer' that day. She asked the ascetic for his bowl so that she would put the kheer in it.

The ascetic showed her the bowl full of dirt. She was going to put the kheer in it, but looked inside it and stopped "Babaji, what have you filled in you bowl!"

"Oh, a little bit of cow dung, sand and dirt is there! What can be done now? You also put the kheer in it."

"I can't babaji. Otherwise the kheer will become filthy. How will you eat it then?" she insisted, "give me the bowl. Let me first wash it clean."

"Oh! You put the kheer in it only after it is cleaned, no?"

"Yes!"

"You see!" the ascetic explained, "This is my advice to you! When your heart is filled with the filth of negative sentiments no advice will do any good. Rather the nectar of good advice will become filthy mixed with it. Therefore eliminate the filth from your heart first!"

Having eliminated this filth we can now groom well the noble qualities: generosity, kindness, sense of sacrifice, humanity, patience and good thoughts.

How can we eliminate the weed of these negative sentiments? Take for example jealousy. Your classmate is chatting with a beautiful girl; you become jealous. At this moment look inside yourself. You are recognizing it! It is there inside you!

Once we recognise the filth we suppress it consciously, "no I will not be envious of my friend!"

When we tell it ourselves a number of times, it will be suppressed and we would prevent ourselves from doing anything negative.

Similarly all the negative sentiments can be wiped out; just it requires self-analysis, self-criticism and the sacrifice of a wrong action.
At this point the seeds of the virtues will start to sprout up and you will have the power to suffocate negative sentiments and not permit them to grow anymore.

With time these negative sentiments will disappear completely from the field of our heart.

Teaching Objective

Discipline, Consistency and love, law of the consequences, sense of logic.

Personality test

- What are the sentiments you must remove from your heart to make it pure?
- What are the sentiments you must cultivate in your heart to live life worth living?
- How are you going to cultivate in yourself friendship, solidarity, altruism, kindness?
- Which are the virtues that you have already sown in your heart?

Questions

a. What did you learn from the story?
b. What does the begging bowl of the ascetic represent in this story?
c. Why did the lady want to clean the begging bowl?
d. What are the qualities in you that you think are like the dirt in the bowl?
e. Have you ever thought of throwing those out of yourself?
f. If yes, what have you done to eliminate those?

Carry out this Exercise

Explain to your friends what the good qualities are and to cultivate them well, how they can eliminate the weeds of bad qualities.

"If a man is determined to do it himself and not to depend on others then the job is obviously done. He will of course come and cut the corns tomorrow morning. Come on, let's fly away to safety!"

How do you want people to behave?

There is he who complains that he is not sufficiently loved by others, that he is neglected and abandoned but without asking himself the reason for all this.

Life gives you that what you give to it, no more and no less. We, therefore, must know ourselves, and make ourselves know what we really are.

Teaching Objective

Interior honesty, self-analysis, strength of will, sacrifice.

Personality Test

- Do you sometimes feel there is no love around you?
- What makes you feel so?
- Does there exist a remedy and what is it?
- Do you think doing things on your own will benefit you?
- In what ways?
- When do you think you are loved the most?

Questions

a. Why did the Saras crane and her children fly away the third time?
b. Why did nobody come to reap the corn first two times?
c. Why did the owner of the field think others did not love him?
d. Have you ever asked your friends to help you?
e. Do you help your friends?
f. When do you think they love you more - when you help them or when they help you?

Carry out this Exercise

Explain how you came to understand that the only cure for not being sad is to open your own heart to others.

The really free man is the slave to his own conscience. This is the RIGHT ACTION 2.11

Teaching Value

Liberty does not mean doing what you wish, but the understanding of what are our rights and together with these our responsibilities and acting in consequence.

Very often, though, we mistake liberty as our exclusive right to do whatever we wish and get whatever we want.

Meme and Mimi were two young goats, living in a small jungle. There was plenty of grass. And no predators were there. It was but obvious that both of them cared none, and lived according to their own rules.

Meme lived this side of the jungle while Mimi lived on the other side, and there was a small river flowing in the middle. And they had never met!

Meme always thought of crossing the river, but how? There were no bridge and the river was deep. Every day he stood on the bank and looked at the green grass on the other side of the river, and cursed his luck.

"How beautiful is the grass there; lush green and thick!" his mouth watered, "Oh dear! I am fed up of eating the same grass every day. Somehow if I can cross the river..!"

One day his wish was fulfilled! An old eucalyptus tree fell due to strong wind, its top touching the other bank!

When Meme saw it he could not resist a moment, and started running over it to the other bank. Then only he saw Mimi - for the first time!

She was coming to this side with the same enthusiasm; she always wandered what is there on the other side.

They stopped and looked at each other. Both were standing just in the middle of the river.

"Get away from here and let me cross it first," shouted Meme.

"Oh! And why should not I cross it first?" Mimi snapped back, "come on you fool, hurry up and run back!"

Meme was angry; he stepped ahead, "I am warning you. If anything happens to you I am not responsible."

Mimi also stepped ahead. Nobody had challenged her so far! "And look at this kid, how dare he come on my way?"

Both had newly grown sharp horns! Both were determined not to give up their rights. Both had temper reached on their heads.

They rose on their hind legs and …thud! ..It was dark all over and so many stars were circling over each one's heads.

The next moment both were in deep waters.

Somehow they reached in the banks, but not on their own side. It was already dusk and the cold water had destroyed their spirit of adventure. They had to return home to the warmth of their mothers.

Both ran back again on the log-bridge, this time from the opposite sides. Again they met each other in the middle.

They looked at each other. This time, though, they understood liberty can kill each other! It was time for compromise.

Suddenly Meme got an idea. He set down on his belly. "Be careful and put your legs on the log on both sides of my body and cross over me," he told Mimi.
Sure enough she crossed over him without any problem.

Now both were happy, just a little compromise and they could do miracles!

Both greeted each other good night and ran towards their home.

Freedom can be of two varieties; physical and interior.

We understood physical liberty now. What is interior liberty?

Well, when you have done your homework and studied, the day after, at school, you have no fears and you feel free. On the other hand when you have not studied you feel anxious and are afraid of the oral test. In this case where the liberty has ended up? On what does it depend? When we have carried out our duty and never before.

To be free signifies having our conscience clear.

Teaching Objective

Responsibility and social conscience, sense of discrimination.
Personality Test

- How do you consider your studies?
  1. A compulsion?
  2. A duty?
  3. A pleasure?
- Do your parents make sacrifices to enable you to study?
- How do you pay them back?
- When do you feel truly free?
- What prevents you from doing every thing you want?
- List what are your rights and your duties.

Questions

a. Why Meme and Mimi had to fight?
b. Do you think they gained greater freedom by compromise? Why?
c. If you were in place of Meme or Mimi, what would you do the second time? Fight for your rights or compromise?
d. What are the rights?
e. What are the duties towards ourselves and towards others?
f. Is it possible not to depend on others?
g. What do you understand by responsibility?

Carry out this Exercise

Have you ever had an experience, at home or among friends, like Mimi and Meme? Note down in detail.

No one is independent. All are interdependent. This is the RIGHT ACTION 2.12

Teaching Value

Society must be considered as a unit whose parts are interdependent.

Man lives in a society where he can develop intelligence and health thanks to the multiple exchanges of food, clothes, education, culture etc.

This gives to man the opportunity to create, dream, and think, and most of all, survive.

Many of us, though, do not believe in team spirit like the yellow bird!

Don't you know the yellow bird? Well, her feathers were golden yellow and shined in the sunshine. She was very proud of herself, and never mixed up with other birds.

One day the woodpecker asked her the reason.

She snapped back, "Don't you see how beautiful I am, and my voice is so sweet. And look at you! How can you ugly birds ask me to mix-up with you?"

Poor woodpecker could not say a word and flew away. All the birds of the jungle had similar experiences. That's why they avoided her.

Then one day she had to face the reality!

The old monkey jumped over her nest and smashed all her eggs. She built another nest and again laid her eggs. After two days he smashed the nest again. Even when she built nests on other trees he followed her and destroyed the nests.

Had the crows been there to protect her, the monkey wouldn't have come; as he was scared of their beaks.

Now he was free to do whatever he wished.

The yellow bird finally went to the king to get justice.

The bear was the king of that small jungle as there were no big animal. The fox was his minister. The king listened to her plead, and gave her a date for judgement. The monkey was also summoned on that date.

On the judgment day the yellow bird again pleaded that the season is almost over and if she could not lay her eggs, there would be no meaning to her life.

The old monkey, in his reply, told the king that it was his birth right to jump on the branches. If the yellowbird suffered she should leave the jungle!

The king was about to speak when the fox interrupted him, "Maharaaj! Please don't take any hurried decision. Elders have advised to look back and forth before giving any judgment. Therefore my lord, please look back."

The bear looked back. And what he finds! A big ripe jackfruit and a large honeycomb behind his throne!

The monkey had sent the gifts through the fox earlier that day.

For days he had not tasted jack fruit. And this big honey comb! Bear's mouth started watering. He immediately understood his minister's hint.

"The monkey is innocent", declared the overjoyed bear, "It is the fault of the Yellowbird. Migratory birds have no right in this jungle. Now go away and don't disturb me again"

Only then the yellow bird realized how lonely she was! What's the use of this beauty if nobody cared for her? Alas! There would be no children of hers this year. How could she bear it?

The crow saw her crying profusely all alone on a branch. "What happened my dear?" she asked. The yellow bird put her head on her shoulder and started crying even more profusely. All her hate for the crow had melted away!

The crow immediately gathered all the birds of the jungle and had a meeting.

When they were discussing the matter in heavy hearts, a sparrow flew in very fast. She was breathing hard, "Dear birds.....", She took her breath, "I have to tell you some thing!"

In fact her nest was on the wall behind the king's throne. She told them about the whole episode. Everyone was shocked! How would they accept such a wicked animal as their king?

The angry crow gave the final verdict, "we are not feeble. They should see the power of our beaks! Come on; right at this moment we'll teach them a lesson"

And she rushed towards the king; the atmosphere was charged with her caw, caw sound. The whole flock followed him everybody with their own kinds of war cry.

The feasting king, his minister and the monkey could not even find time to understand what was happening! So vicious the attack was that neither of the three had a single fur left on their bodies!

You would have enjoyed taking photographs of the fleeing trio, completely exposed!!

They have never returned back again.

Teaching Objective

Social conscience, cooperation

Personality Test

- Are you happier when you are alone or when you are in company?
- If you don't succeed in doing something alone what do you do?
  1. Ask for help?
  2. give up?
  3. Get somebody else to do it?
- What does your school give to you?
- Have you ever used the services of the baker, of the police, of the Red Cross..?
- Do you think you will survive without the help of the society? Why?

Questions

a. Why the yellow bird liked to stay alone?
b. Why did the other birds stay away from her?
c. In what way can we help one another?
d. How many things can we do by helping one another?
e. What does your school give to you?
f. Have you ever noticed that while you sleep others work for you?
g. Who are they?

Carry out this Exercise

Show how it is possible to pay our debt to the society now or later on.

Science without humanity is useless and Dangerous. This is the RIGHT ACTION 2.13

Teaching Value

Most of us understand this today, don't we? Unchecked scientific development has caused destruction of forest covers, and numerous rare plants and animals. Weapons of mass destruction have been produced in the name of security and are being used against innocent people. The green house effect in the atmosphere is slowly becoming a threat for survival. The rapid change of climate is frequent now, causing loss of human lives.

Intuition, curiosity, constancy, perseverance and most of all altruism are the qualities of a great scientist.

Unfortunately most of the scientists forget altruism and love for nature and life. Selfishness and greed makes them invent dangerous and useless things.

Not to forget that they are just like the frog king who had a serpent friend!

The frog king lived inside a deserted well and ruled over the few frogs that resided there. There were plenty of insects to feed all of them. All lived in peace and tranquility. Slowly the frog king grew old. Only a few respected him now.

When you feel old and you no longer can do the job, you must find a well deserving person to do it. But the frog king was greedy of power. Instead he decided the other way around.

One day he secretly came out of the well and went to a deadly cobra, who lived inside an anthill nearby.

He called upon the cobra. When the cobra came out, he told him how his subjects were disrespecting him.

"Why don't we become friends dear cobra?" he emphasized, "You come with me and reside inside the well. I'll show you who my dissidents are. Just have your fill! This way you and I will live peacefully. Only condition is don't ever touch my family and friends."

The cobra readily followed him to the well.

And one by one he ate away all his dissidents and their families. Now of course the frog was the undisputed ruler.

The serpent, however, ate few of his friends next day. When the king complained, he said, "Sir, now that your dissidents are no more how I would fill my stomach? It's your duty to feed me."

The poor frog put his head down and returned back silently. While the cobra kept on eating his friends he behaved as if he does not know a thing. Soon it was the turn of his family members.

Now only he realized the fatality of his plan. But things were already out of his hands. He just waited for the day when his turn will come…

Therefore the people who handle great knowledge and technologies must be altruist and benevolent towards all. Otherwise they themselves will never escape their deeds.

You know very often scientists have to work against all odds including incredulity and even the hostility of people. All the great inventers had to face such situations in life.

In the dark moments we survive if we have an unshakable determination towards general well being, and a belief in the progress of humanity.

Finally, we must develop love for the nature within ourselves.

Teaching Objective

Love of nature, curiosity, force of will, desire for knowledge, perseverance, success and failure, altruism.

Personality Test

- Do you like looking at nature?
- Have you ever noticed there are many inventions which are dangerous for nature?
- How did you know that they are dangerous?
  1. From your teacher or parents
  2. From books and magazines
  3. Through television
- Do you have the curiosity to discover the reason why for all things?
- Have you ever made experiments?
- What are the qualities that you must have to become a scientist?

Questions

a. Do you think the frog king was intelligent? Why?
b. What made him think of such an evil plan?
c. What was the result of it?
d. What are the scientific inventions and discoveries that are destroying the nature?
e. How can we survive from it?
f. What are the inventions that you think are nature friendly?

Carry out this Exercise

Tell an episode, drawn from the life of a great scientist, in which the human values are underlined.

Peace

Eliminate the "I" and Peace will remain. This is PEACE 3.1

Teaching Value

Peace depends on the interior equilibrium of each one of us, which we obtain by practicing moral living. We already know from the last two sections what moral living is. Yet I'll tell you another story.

The name of the story is "Man - Made of Soil".

How true! What are we? What is this body made of the natural elements such as air, water, minerals, etc. When we die our body dissolves in these natural elements.

What is left then? Nothing is there which I can call "my" this or "my" that. Understanding this fact only will help us eliminate the "I" and lead us to inner peace!

They were two brothers; with an age gap of ten years. Their father, a well respected but poor farmer had told them while dying, "Never divide the property."

The elder brother was a very upright man and was equally well respected. He had a caring wife and four children - three daughters and a son. The younger brother was a happy-go-lucky guy. Never too serious about earning, he spent most of the time in extracurricular activities. The children loved him very much. What a happy family they were living together in joys and sorrows until the younger brother got married!

The new bride was from a rich family. As she had brought valuable ornaments, several utensils, silk cloths, etc. as gifts for this poor family she wanted every thing according to her own convenience. Her elder sister-in-law did not like that as she was losing her powers over the family. Now their egos clashed frequently resulting in smalltime quarrels. And in the nights both would convey their respective husbands what derogatory remarks the other sister-in-law had made.

While the elder brother, with his mental peace intact, suggested his wife to try and tolerate, the younger brother was too scared of his elder brother to complain any thing.

Slowly, though, their relationship started deteriorating. Once when the elder brother overheard the two sisters-in-law quarreling, he called upon his wife and told her never to respond to the younger sister-in-law's harsh words. "If again I hear you quarreling I'll leave this home at once," he threatened her.

Yet another day he overheard their quarrel and sure enough left the home!

Then only his wife realized that her fights were worthless. What was she fighting for and for whom? Was it for herself? Then why was she feeling wretched without her husband? Was it for her husband? But he was happy when she was not fighting!

She was loved when she made sacrifices! And it was love that she wanted!

After much request by the villagers when he returned home after seven days she promised to take care of the whole family as lovingly as before - with her newfound conscience!

The younger sister-in-law became more jealous now, because her elder counterpart could not be provoked. With her heart burning, she kept on coaxing her husband, "look at them, how happy they are, they got their daughters married with all your money! They are making a fool of you! And you are an idiot not to ask for division of property." She had lots of dreams about how they would enjoy living alone, spend according to their wish and live like rich people. Naturally easy going, he also dreamt through the eyes of his beautiful wife.

Still the fear of elder brother prevented him from asking for division.

That year the elder brother got the last of his daughters married. He took care not to spend at least half of the year's products, as there might be a dispute. Yet the younger sister-in-law could not believe in the uprightness of the elder brother. She made her husband believe that his brother had kept some secret funds, half of which should have been theirs. The younger brother believed her readily and thought of getting the property divided immediately. He invited the crooked landlord to be witness of their division of property.

Next morning the landlord came to their home with a false benevolent smile, and asked the elder brother to start dividing the property right away. The elder brother failed to understand, as he had no idea about the younger brother's decision. When he learnt about his intentions, at first he drove away the landlord telling that it was their internal matter and he didn't need his help.

After the grumbling landlord went away he asked his brother to sit near him, "Our late father wanted this property to remain undivided. Isn't it?"

"Yes,..but!", the younger brother was agitated, "but I need my half of the property!"

"OK. You want property and I want it undivided. We both have our wishes fulfilled!" He smiled at his younger brother.

Then he called his wife, "Come dear. Now that I have decided to leave all the property for my younger brother, let's go. And mind you, don't take any thing other than our two changes of cloth." His wife understood him well. She knew that her husband is all that matters to her. And when they were together, they could face any situation. She bundled up clothes and took their son by hand, and all the three slowly went out of the home.

The younger brother was watching spellbound. He didn't know what to do. His father like brother and mother like sister-in-law were leaving him....for what? For this earthen house, these wooden furniture, these utensils...? Where is the soul in these? Where is life, where is love in these lifeless things.. are these the wealth he always craved for? He could not think further.

Next morning he was squatting in front of a door five miles away; the door of the home that had given refuse to his elder brother for a day. When the family came out of the house for further journey he went up to his brother.

"Brother, please take me along!"

"Where?"

"Wherever you go!"

The elder brother could see the earnestness and love in his eyes!

"Come!" He smiled, "let's go home."

The heart, in which the moral sense is housed, is always an inspirer of good actions and only in this way will our life be balanced and useful to ourselves, our family, our country, and the whole world.

A great deal of peace in the household depends on the woman.

Teaching Objective

Interdependence between the values, emotions, desires, self control, wisdom.

Personality Test

- When you are at peace do you feel free?
- According to you, how is it possible to have a peaceful class at school?
- What sacrifices do you have to make to obtain peace?
- Can you obtain peace by demanding it from someone?
- Why, if I do not have peace within myself, can I neither have it externally?

Questions

a. Who is in peace in this story? Why?
b. What advice did the elder brother give to his wife?
c. Is wealth permanent?
d. Can one take along any thing when he dies?
e. On what does peace depend?

Carry out this Exercise

Give examples of the times in which you have lost your peace for having said or done a wrong action.

The greatest show of power is calm. This is PEACE 3.2

Teaching Value

To be calm, satisfied with what we have, accepted our own limits and the problems of the others, respect others, to have the capacity of concentration, to use our possessions correctly, have patience, to have the capacity to look at the events and circumstances to draw right conclusions are the qualities that denote a peaceful person.

India, the second largest democracy in the world, is such a wonderful place to live! Our this secular nation has given us ample freedom to live as we like and do what we wish to do irrespective of our cast, creed and religion. In fact our political setup is one of the most democratic setups in the world and our judicial system is amongst the most tolerating.

All this is possible only because we are a free nation!

And the man who spearheaded our freedom struggle is non-other than Mahatma Gandhi the foremost promoter of peace and non-violence. Gandhiji in true sense personified the saying "The greatest show of power is calm."
Don't you believe this? Well, let us consider one of the famous happenings in his life.

Once while he was traveling first class in a train in South Africa, the ticket collector threw him out of the compartment only because he was not a white man.

He did not scream foul language at the ticket collector or hit him back; neither did he cry for this disrespect. With his inner peace intact, he carefully decided to fight back. And we all know how he fought in South Africa as well as in India.

And what was the result? Within a few years he brought down the whole British Empire to its knees. What a display of power!

From where did such enormous power come to such a frail man like him the man who wore only a loin cloth and lived a simple life? It came from his inner strength because his peaceful mind radiated all the positive energies.

Gandhiji always said, "Show him the other cheek if somebody slaps you on one cheek!"

Did he mean you surrender to him? No!

What he actually meant was convey to your opponent that you are not scared of him, but he is scared of you your inner strength. When you react in this way he feels he is powerless, and he gets bewildered, frustrated. Obviously he is defeated in his own hands!

See what your inner peace could achieve!

India's freedom itself is the proof of this calmness what we could not achieve in bloody fights; we achieved it without raising our hands on anybody!

The peace, therefore, is attained starting from the individual to reach the masses, and not the other way around.

Teaching Objective

Interior balance.

Personality Test

- When do you lose your calm?
- When are you satisfied with yourself?
- When you act do you first always think of what is right and what is wrong?
- Do you intervene to defend a companion who is weaker than you?
- Are you able to impose discipline on yourself?

Questions

a. What do you know about Gandhi?
b. Do you think he did not fight the ticket collector because he was scared of him?
c. What did Gandhi wear?
d. Do you know what his clothes represent?
e. Do you believe in his saying "show him the other cheek if somebody slaps you on one cheek!"
f. If yes, why?
g. If no, why?

Carry out this Exercise

How can you contribute to the peace of the world?

Patience is the virtue of the strong.
This is PEACE 3.3

Teaching Value

Patience is a component of peace that denotes the wisdom of he who knows how to wait. What is necessary is to have the patience to wait; the marvel of life will show itself to our eyes.

Here is a story which tells us how the great patience of a King and Queen turned away evil from their country and their race.

There was once a King called Kushika. He was a good ruler. His citizens were happy and he lived a peaceful life.

But the great Rishi Chyavana, by the powers of his yoga got to know that a descendent of Kusika's race would destroy numerous Brahmins. "I must kill the king and the queen so that nobody will ever be born of them," he thought and went to the court of the king.

But so long as no fault could be found with the King or his wife he could do them no injury.

So Chyavana thought of a plan.

He said to the king, "I wish to observe a certain vow, and during that period you and your wife shall serve me." The King and Queen accepted gladly and treated him well with royal food. After food, Chyavana said, "I need to sleep. So you and your wife press my feet until I get up. And mind you, never disturb me in my sleep." The King said "so be it" and he and the Queen kept on pressing his feet without fatigue.

Chyavana slept for twenty-one days. Then he rose and went out of the room without speaking to them. The king and Queen, tired and hungry, followed him, but he would not even look at them, and at last he suddenly disappeared, for he was a great Yogi and had the power to make himself invisible.

The King and Queen were full of grief and began to look everywhere for the Rishi, and at last returned to the palace only thinking about him. They went to the palace and there they found the Rishi on his bed. Once more they took their seats and began to press his feet, and he slept another twenty-one days.

Then he awoke and said, "Rub my body with oil, I wish to have a bath." The King and Queen did as the Rishi asked for a long time, and at last he went into the bathing room and again disappeared.

Nothing however disturbed the King and Queen, and very soon they found the Rishi seated on the throne. Then they gave him all kinds of good and excellent food, but instead of eating it, the Rishi set fire to it all, and burnt it to ashes. Yet the King was not angry, but served the Rishi day and night.

The Rishi was very upset seeing his plans fail. This time he was harder on the King, "I want to visit your kingdom. You and your wife pull my chariot instead of the horses. Also load it with lots of gems and Wealth so that I can bestow upon your citizens."

The king said "So be it" and he and his wife did accordingly. The people and the ministers of the King followed the car, and were in great grief to see their King and Queen in such condition.

The Rishi struck the King and Queen with his goad, but they were still patient in their service and bore him along, although their wound bled and they were worn out with toil and hunger.

The great Rishi could not see the sufferings of such fine human beings any more. He changed his mind and stopped the car. Then he got down and released the King and the Queen.

With tears in his eye he said, "Great is your virtue, and because of your great patience I am very much pleased with you". Then he softly touched their bodies with his hands and healed all their wounds and they felt no longer tired or hungry. Also with his yogic powers he made their kingdom full of wealth and prosperity.

Chyavana blessed them for a long life and disappeared.

In this way the good King and Queen, by their great patience, love and duty saved their race and country from destruction.

In this life there are many evils, which easily take away our peace. But patience can turn the evil into good enabling us not to lose our peace.

Teaching Objective

Patience, faith in ourselves, perseverance, serenity.

Personality Test

- According to you, what does being patient depend on?:
  1. On your will?
  2. On faith?
  3. On perseverance?
  4. On hurry?
  5. On the desire to succeed?
- With patience do you think you can overcome every obstacle?
- Are you able to wait patiently for your turn in a queue?
- To be patient, does this mean to be strong or weak?

Questions

a. Why did Rishi Chyavana want to kill the King and the queen?
b. Did he succeed in his intentions?
c. What made the king Kushika and his Queen pass the test with flying colours?
d. What this story teaches other than patience?

Carry out this Exercise

Tell from your past experience how patience helped you?

Our greatest virtue is not to fall. But to rise again every time we fall. This is the PEACE 3.4.

Teaching Value

Perseverance is a component of the value of peace.

The will which guides us in carrying out an enterprise to finish at all costs the things which we start and projects. Mode is the will for the research.

Maharaaj Sukarna Singh was a very good ruler indeed. He looked after the needs of the poor and respected the wise. The impact was visible in his kingdom. Yet the king was a very humble man and always wanted to learn more. He was, therefore, in need of a good 'Rajguru' or the royal adviser.

Once so happened that a great sage was traveling through his kingdom. He had settled down in the jungle at the outskirts of the city.

For years the king had nourished the desire to meet him. With immense happiness he went to meet the sage.

When he reached there he was surprised to see the sage prostrating against a small bush. It seemed so funny to the king.

"What is he doing...", he asked himself.

The saint got up after a while and took his seat. The king greeted him with respect and expressed his curiosity.

He asked him to come closer, "Come here, your majesty, and look - what is that?"

A spider was weaving its web upon the bush!

"It's just a spider! But sir, why would you prostrate in front of an insignificant spider?" the king asked.

The sage smiled, "It has taught me a vital fact of life. Therefore it has gained a respectable place as a Guru for me."

"What is that you have learned, O enlightened?" the king was more curious then ever.

The sage explained, "Since this morning I am observing this spider. As you see it is on the verge of completing this magnificent spider-web. Do you know how it began to weave its first thread?

Countless times the thread broke down as it was crossing to the next bush. It would fall on the ground mid way. Without any delay it crawled back to the bush, then to the top of the branch, and then it reworked again on the thread. Every time it fell it started again with more zeal. Now look, how he has succeeded finally!

My dear king, this is what is called Perseverance. Fail as many times as you may, but never stop pursuing your goal."

The king had gained such an important lesson that day.

Every enterprise, be it small, that we enter into requires this component of peace. It does not matter if you don't succeed in an undertaking but the importance is to have done everything possible.

Teaching Objective

Self-analysis and force of will.

Personality Test

- In what field of activity do you feel you are most persevering:
1. In games?
2. In your studies?
3. In your hobbies?
- What do you think of a person who abandons an undertaking at the first difficulty?
- When, at school, you don't understand the lesson do you ask for it to be repeated or do you let the matter drop?
- If you get bad marks do you get discouraged or do you dedicate yourself even more?
- Do you take part in some sporting activity? Watch yourself and show your perseverance.

Questions

a. Have you ever noticed how the spider weaves its web?
b. Why the sage thought of the spider as his Guru?
c. What did he tell the king?
d. Is it possible for man to succeed in any undertaking whatsoever?
e. What relation is there between peace and perseverance?
f. What relation is there between will and perseverance?

Carry out this Exercise

Tell how a famous person has reached his goal as a result of perseverance.

What you think of yourself is much more important then what others think of you. This is PEACE 3.5

Teaching Value

Joke goes:

Once Pundit Jawaharlal Nehru attended an annual day celebration of a madhouse. A man was being released on that day and the superintendent thought it would be good if Prime Minister release him by his own hand. So the man was brought out.

Jawaharlal Nehru asked him, "How long have you been here?"

He said, "Three years, and these people are very good. They have cured me absolutely."

Then suddenly he asked, "But who are you?"

"Don't you know me?" Punditjee said, "I am Pundit Jawaharlal Nehru, Prime Minister of India."

The man said, "Don't be worried. These people will cure you within three years. That's what I used to think when I came here. I suffered from the same trouble."

How true, although a joke!

Everybody thinks of you from his own perspective. Therefore never judge yourselves by what others say of you. Then you lose your mental peace.

Shyam was not a good student. His classmates, therefore, ridiculed him; teachers thrashed him and parents scolded him almost every day. In return he felt frustrated, did mischief deliberately and never listened to anybody.

One day the new sports teacher noticed him standing outside the class as math teacher had punished him. The sports teacher had a good glance at Shyam's healthy body from a distance; he felt a good sportsman in the making.

That afternoon, he called him and asked how he had made such a good physic.

"Oh! Everyday I slip away from home early and swim in the nearby pond for an hour, sir. But don't tell it to my class teacher. Always I come late to the class and he would beat me if he knows the reason"

Next day the sports teacher went to the pond early and observed him swim. He was a very good swimmer indeed.

He called him afterwards and told, "Shyam you are an excellent swimmer. Don't be ashamed for yourself and concentrate on swimming. But I want you to be the champion in the interstate school sports."

"Sir," he said with conviction, "this is what I can do the best. Therefore I promise I will never let you down."

That year when he became the champion, all of his classmates wanted to be his friends, teachers praised him and parents told others happily about their son's achievements. He now stopped doing mischief and did reasonably well in the exams.

Now you see, when Shyam got to know himself how the opinion of the same people around him changed!

When someone discovers his own merits and defects he acquires more confidence in himself, having higher esteem of himself and accepting more easily the defects of others.

Hence by knowing ourselves and loving ourselves we learn how to love others, which in turn leads us in to peace and happiness.

Teaching Objective

Interior honesty, self analysis, love of the truth.

Personality Test

- Do you help others?
- Do you wait your turn or do you push in front of others?
- Do you copy your exercises from others?
- Do you recognise your errors?
- When you find something do you return to its legitimate owner?

Questions

a. What does the joke on Pundit Jawaharlal Nehru mean?
b. Why did Shyam gets thrashing from his parents and teachers?
c. What did he like to do best?
d. Why do you think when he became a swimming champion he did less mischief?
e. What does self-analysis mean and what is its usefulness?
f. Have you the capacity to recognise also the negative part that lives in you?
g. Would you be able to punish yourself for a bad action?

Carry out this Exercise

Demonstrate how self-analysis helps you to understand yourself.

Necessity shines the wits.
This is PEACE 3.6

Teaching Value

Curiousity is at the bottom of all human progress. It is only because he was driven by an insatiable curiosity that man has been able to discover and invent; thus passing from caves to the pile dwellings, to the wheel, to the boat and so on up to the rocket, laser rays and computers.

But curiosity can sometimes get us into the trouble. However with good will and perseverance we will be able to pull ourselves out of it in the end without too much damage.

The mouse was very curious. Always he wanted to know new things. One day he visited his uncle's house that was a hole just below the lion's cave. And the lion happened to be the king of the jungle.

The mouse had never seen a lion before. He became so curious that he decided to have a close look at him that day only. When everybody was having afternoon nap, he slipped away and went up into the cave.

The lion was also snoring in the cool of the cave. At first he watched this magnificent creature with wonder and awe from a safe distance. But the snore of the lion encouraged him. He climbed up its tail slowly and then went on looking allover its body. He was so thrilled!

When he touched it's whiskers, the lion woke up, and in a flash of a second the mouse was in its powerful claws.

"You little creature," the lion roared with anger, "how dare you climb up my body? I'll crash my claws over the floor and watch your blood sprinkling away."

But the mouse did not lose his cool, "I beg your pardon, Sir!" he told with courtesy, "I am just a little mouse, and a foreigner. And I must congratulate you, for all the animals of my jungle are your fan. They say you are a true king and a large hearted one. But…"

"But what?" The lion roared again.

"Some body has spread rumors that your mouth stinks. All my mice friends are depressed, because they think your mouth has fragrance of wild flowers.

I told them not to worry and promised to take a strand of your whisker which carries the fragrance of your mouth, may it cost what...after all you are our idol.

Since I have seen and touched you, therefore I have no desire to live anymore. I'll be happy to die in your hands....only that your majesty's reputation can not be reestablished." The mouse took a deep breath and sighed aloud.

Thoroughly mollified by now, the lion gave one of its whiskers and freed him!

I guess you know the rest of the story about how the mouse saved the lion.

Now we may think why curiosity is a component of the value of peace? Because we cannot be at peace unless our curiosity becomes satisfied.

And it is curiosity of man that has led him to search ceaselessly both inside and outside of himself to reach the great truths of morality and religion.

The proverbs connected with this panel are:

1. Don't ever despair!
2. He who stops is lost.
3. When a door is closed a window is opened up!

Teaching Objective

Curiosity and perseverance.

Personality Test

- Are you curious?
- When you are in trouble what do you do:
    1. Ask help of others?
    2. Look for a solution by yourself?
    3. Give up?
- Do you know how to control your curiosity with prudence and attention?

Questions

a. Can curiosity get us into trouble?
b. What is necessary to get out of trouble?
c. Does every experience teach something new?
d. What relationship is there between the story and the value of "peace"?
e. What is faith in ourselves?
f. Do you think you can learn something new every day?
g. Do you think there may be limit to human curiosity?

Carry out this Exercise

Recount a negative experience that has taught you something.

Recognise your own errors.
You are pardoned by half. This is PEACE 3.7

Teaching Value

Avoiding our own responsibilities and putting the blame on others is an attitude which is very common and not confined only to the young but also among adults. This attitude always causes loss of inner peace afterwards.

The man who is really strong is he who admits his own errors and accepts his responsibilities.

Perhaps you are thinking when you grow up and become a 'man' you would be strong.

No Sir, strength has to be cultivated right at your age.

Young Lal Bahadur was just a little kid of six years. One day some of his schoolmates planned to steal guavas from a nearby guava plantation. It seemed pretty adventurous. Lal Bahadur also accompanied them.

They crossed the fence clandestinely and climbed the trees; and all of them had lot of fun.

Soon the guard, a ferocious looking man with a heavy club in his hand, heard their sound and ran towards them shouting like a mad man.

They quickly jumped down from the trees and ran as fast as they could. Within no time all of them had crossed the fences; all but Lal Bahadur.

By now he had realized that he had done a wrong thing and he should face the consequences. Although very much scared he stood there calmly. The guard came like a raging bull and stopped near him. "You little brat," he flashed his red eyes and screamed, "I'll break your legs this moment so that you can never dare to enter here again."

Lal Bahadur stood in front of him head down, prepared for punishment.

The guard looked at him, thought for a while and then said in a calm but commanding voice, "OK, I am leaving you this time. But remember, stealing is a crime. Never do it again."

The kid nodded and returned back. And never in his life he did any thing foul again!

Yes you remember correctly, he is none other then one of our most honest Prime Ministers, the Late Lal Bahadur Shastri, the little man who showed his guts both in war and in peace.

On the contrary, when we get bad marks, very often we blame the teacher who does not know how to evaluate us; or it is our little brother or sister who has disturbed us and hasn't let us study, or our parents, and on other occasions even time "....there was no time to study...".

This character defect, if we allow it to grow, will accompany us up to maturity compromising our capacity to grow up and assume our own responsibilities. In fact the grown-ups very often say: "The fault is that of the government's, of society, of our parents who when we were small haven't taught this or that and so finish by making a mistake..."

But in realty the fault is only our own! This is one of the reasons why we never find peace.

Teaching Objectives

Interior honesty, self-analysis, self-criticism as a discipline for eliminating grave defects of character.

Personality Test

- Do you also give the blame to others when you make a mistake?
- Do you feel all right when you try to hide your error?
- Do you feel stronger when you recognise you have made a mistake?
- Do you always feel responsible for the actions you do?

Questions

a. What do you know about Lal Bahadur Shastri?
b. What would you do if you were in place of young Lal Bahadur?
c. Do you need a great deal of strength to admit your own errors?
d. Why is honesty towards ourselves and self-criticism linked to the value of peace?

Carry out this Exercise

How many times do we give the blame to someone in the society, the family or in school! Give several examples of this and demonstrate the uselessness of the action.

Discipline and honesty are like your shadow, inseparable from you. This is PEACE 3.8

Teaching Value

Discipline and honesty are the two elements for living correctly and safely, without which there cannot be peace.

Discipline means learning to keep ourselves healthy and clean; obey the rules laid down for living together usefully and peacefully in school as in society; punctuality, to keep in order your desk like you would at home, not to throw things on the ground, etc.

Honesty means being faithful to the truth and knowing our own limits and respecting them. Without interior honesty, that towards ourselves, there cannot be exterior honesty, that towards others.

THE DOVE KING

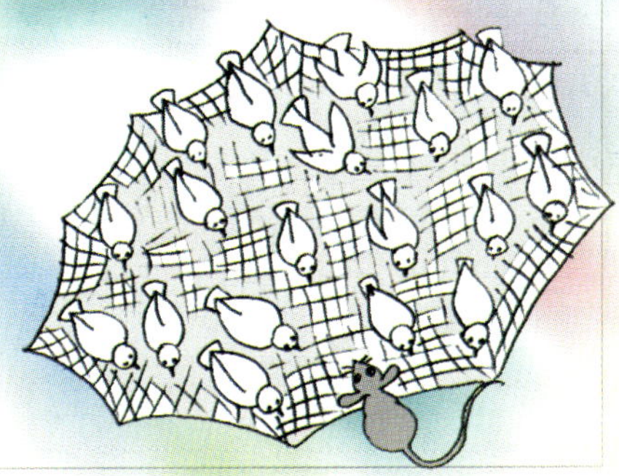

The dove king had a small company of doves. All of them were honest and disciplined. Therefore they lived together peacefully in the jungle.

Then one day a hunter came and threw grains of rice and corns in an open field. He put a trap of thin strong threads over the field and went away for a midday nap.

From high in the sky the doves saw food spread over the field, but they could not see the net.

Immediate greed for food shattered their discipline for a moment and they began diving towards the ground.

The dove king tried to stop them, "No! Don't be so impatient; these grains are not the product of jungle. There must be some trick behind it!" he tried to explain.

But greed had shattered their honesty as well! "Look at this selfish king," they thought, "he is preventing us from eating such delicious food. Whom is he fooling? When we go away, he will come alone and eat away all these grains."

They landed on the ground disobeying the king; and stuck themselves in the net.

The dove king, though, was very honest. When he saw his subjects struggling for freedom he could not resist himself and landed straight in the trap among them.

His sacrifice humbled the doves. They felt ashamed for their dishonesty and indiscipline. Things are out of their control now. The hunter would kill them in a few moments! They cried in great sorrow.

But the wise dove king did not lose his cool. He calmed the wailing doves. "Listen to me carefully!" he told them, "I have a mouse friend who lives in the far corner of this jungle. He can cut the net and free us. But the question is how we reach there....

Only one thing can be done. When I say 1..2..3..go, each of us would flap our wings simultaneously with all the energy. And start flying to the direction of the mouse at the same time.

And never break the discipline. If any of us breaks it, this heavy net will pull us down and every body will die."

They followed his orders and flapped simultaneously. To their disbelief the heavy and big net slowly got lifted from the ground!

When the cruel hunter came to kill the doves nothing was there except a few grains on the ground!

That day they had learned one thing- never disregard honesty and discipline; even for a moment.

These are the rules that we must learn to face up to all the events and circumstances of life. For example, we impose upon ourselves certain dietetic rules to keep us in good health, if we transgress them this will cause us physical damage.

Hence we must learn the concepts of discipline and honesty to learn to act right.

Teaching Objective

Discipline and honesty.

Personality Test

- Is it possible to learn anything without discipline?
- If you have no honesty towards yourself can you have it towards others?
- Can you learn discipline in a day?
- Give examples of the professions, which require discipline.
- If you were not to follow the rules of the game would you be able to win a game of cricket?

Questions

a. Do you like the story of the Dove king? Why?
b. Why did the doves get into trouble?
c. Why did the dove king put himself in the trap?
d. What would you do if you were the dove king?
e. What would have been the consequences if one of the doves had broken the rule?
f. Why can't you face up to the dangers of life without honesty and discipline?
g. Must we be honest everywhere and in all occasions?

Carry out this Exercise

Enlist the rules you would follow were you staying in a hostel.

Where there is a will there is a way.
This is PEACE 3.9

Teaching Value

The malicious traits of character and the dangerous signs that inflame the heart are, anger, hate, selfishness, greed, pride and self-interest.

These vices of the character are the fierce enemies of the man, which always make him cause severe damage to himself and others. And peace is lost!

Don't you know the story of the mongoose?

Well, it was a loving pet of a family of three persons, a husband, his wife and their newborn baby boy.

Once when the husband was away from home on some work, the lady left the mongoose to play with the baby and went to the pond to fetch water. In the mean time a deadly cobra entered the room and approached the child raising its hood.

It was on the verge of biting the baby when the mongoose noticed it. He straightaway jumped over it and struck its hood. Leaving the baby alone the cobra hissed at the mongoose furiously. And they had a vicious fight. Finally the mongoose killed the cobra and tore it into pieces.

Happy and full of self-pride, it ran to the pond to express its feelings to the lady.

When she saw it running to her with a bloody mouth she thought it had killed her baby. Blind with sudden anger she crashed the pitcher full of water on it and ran home wailing for her baby.

By the time she realized her mistake the mongoose already had lost its life!

While the self-pride of the mongoose caused it's loss of life, the anger of the lady made her lose the benevolent mongoose.

Therefore we should never fall prey to negative emotions.

Look at the following pictures. In the first picture flames of negative emotions devour the heart: anger, hate, selfishness, greed, pride and self-interest. Look at the expression of the heart.

To prevent them and put them out there is no other way but practice of the human values of truth, the right action, peace, love and non-violence.

As in the second picture we see the four fire hoses of truth, love, peace and the right action extinguishing the fire. Look how the expression of the heart has changed!

How do we change the negative emotions in day-to-day life?

Somebody said to put out the flame of anger it was sufficient to drink a glass of water. Yet somebody said we must start counting fingers one, two, three,... and so on. And then somebody suggested laughing aloud.

Did you ever think of these? Try these yourselves!

Always remember that to let ourselves be overcome by anger or rage is always to be discouraged.

Teaching Objective

How to extinguish passion, force of will, firmness.

Personality Test

- What colour do you become when you get angry?
- What do you understand by "the fire of passions"?
- What is the most suitable name for the captain of your squad of fireman: 1. Force of will, 2. Faith, 3. Courage, 4. Discipline?
- When a companion pulls your leg do you succeed in controlling yourself?
- When your rage has calmed down do you feel guilty?
- When a friend gets angry do you make an effort to calm him down?

Questions

a. Why did the mongoose get killed?
b. Was it only the fault of the lady?
c. Was it the fault of the mongoose alone?
d. What would you do if you were in place of the lady?
e. How does a fire occur?
1. All of a sudden and becomes immediately large?
2. From little spark which propagates slowly?
f. How do you put out a fire?

Carry out this Exercise

Tell of an episode when you were able to extinguish the fire of your heart.

Healthy in Mind healthy in body. This is the PEACE 3.10

Teaching Value

The laugh is very important for the health of our bodies just as it is for moral health.

But princess Saubhagyalaxmi never believed in it. She was a little princess of your age and, was the only child of King Aryamaan. Just that she did not laugh.

Most of us laugh at the cost of others. For example, when Kamlesh slipped on a banana skin, me, Sadhna and Rupesh had a hearty laugh. Next day, Kamlesh took revenge by laughing at me all day because he saw a street dog chasing me and I was running for my life.

We all laugh over such acts, don't we?

But the princess did not laugh!

It's because she had no friends. The king had employed all kinds of jokers and entertainers to make her laugh. And everybody tried such funny acts. They tried their level best. Every day she watched several jokers almost as a routine work, and detested watching it.

She was thoroughly bored of such deliberate buffoonery. That's why, with days passing, she felt gloomier and her health deteriorated accordingly.

The king tried every medicine possible but nothing worked. She even avoided meeting people and liked to stay alone. This made the king, the queen and the whole palace gloomy.

One day the princess slipped away from her room unnoticed and, was walking along the far corner of the royal garden when she noticed a little girl crying aloud. She was, in fact, the two-year-old daughter of her maidservant. Her mother was busy working in the palace. The child had come away this far unknowingly, and could not find her way back among the bushes.

Princess Saubhagyalaxmi was irritated at first. Then finding nobody around her, she started to console the child, but in vain. Finally she remembered a clown's deliberate fall, and fell like him on the grass making funny sounds.

The child noticed and smiled a little. Then again she started crying. The princess did a monkey roll and made faces. She laughed at her. Then she slapped herself and fell again. The child laughed again.

The princess did more such acts and the girl laughed more and more until her mother, the maidservant came looking for her child.

The princess herself was so happy that she smiled at her!

The maidservant, pleasantly surprised by her smile, ran as fast as she could to tell the Queen and the king.

Now she had found out the secret of her happiness: her happiness lied in making others happy!

With days passed, she tried to make her parents and the people around happy, and she became happier then ever. This had a positive impact on her health and her parents' health too.

Slowly the whole kingdom became a happy and prosperous kingdom!

You know what science tells us about laughter?

Laughing enlarges the diaphragm and fills the lungs. The liver is massaged and quantities of the bile are produced. Circulation of blood accelerates and the glands increase their secretions. The thyroid, the pancreas and the suprarenal glands are stimulated together with the gland at the base of the brain.

Check with your science teacher how all these physical phenomena work to build up a healthy body!

The bottom line is why worry unnecessarily for the future! Let's laugh away at ourselves, and make others happy; and live the present to its full extent.

Teaching Objective

Sense of humour, relationship of mind to body.

Personality Test

- Are you more amused:
  1. When you laugh at yourself?
  2. When you laugh at others?
- Laughing gives health:
  1. To the body?
  2. To the mind?
  3. To both of them?
- Do you think you have a sense of humour?
- What relationship is there between the capacity to laugh and the value of peace?
- Does he who laughs make us feel more secure?
- Do you find yourself more at ease with cheerful companions?

Questions

a. Why was the princess unhappy?
b. Why her parents the king and the queen were unhappy?
c. What made her laugh?
d. What is a sense of humour?
e. Can humour make you healthier?
f. Why does a sense of humour make friendship easier?

Carry out this Exercise

The body is a marvelous machine; explain how every organ and every function of these organs are interdependent?

He who is a slave of his desires is a slave of the world. This is PEACE 3.11

Teaching Value

To be able to become masters of our mind we must understand its working. Don't you think so? Most important of all we must know how our desires have made us slaves!

Let me tell you the story of Sage Valmiki, oh! I am sorry, the story of Dashyu Ratnakar.

Dashyu Ratnakar was a very dangerous robber. He intimidated the travelers and pilgrims in the middle of a dense forest and murdered them before looting all their valuables. He, therefore, managed to live a lavish life along with a beautiful wife and loving children, all enjoying the riches he had acquired. His old parents were also party to it. His friends and neighbours praised him.

Then one day he intimidated an old Brahmin in the jungle. The saint was on pilgrimage with few of his disciples.

He asked Dashyu Ratnakar, "But, you will acquire great sin along with the wealth you would collect by killing us, don't you know that?"

"Yes I know, but I am not enjoying the loot alone; my family and friend share it. Why should I acquire it alone? They will also share my sins happily!"

"Ha..ha..ha", laughed the Brahmin, "you are so hopeful of them. Why don't just go and ask them?"

"Are you kidding?" said dashyu Ratnakar angrily, "I'll go ask them and you'll run away, no?"

"No, I will wait till you return. This is the word of a Brahmin," he reiterated, "Just go and ask your wife, children, parents and friends if they would share your sins as they have shared your earnings?"

He went straight to his wife and asked her.

"My dear," she replied, "I am your wife. My job is to keep you satisfied and grow your children. I am doing my duty honestly. In return it is your responsibility to look after me. Since I never demanded so much of wealth why, then, I must be a party to your sins?"

Frustrated, he asked his parents the same.

They wanted to save themselves, "Dear son, we gave birth to you and nourished you well. Now it is your duty to look after us. We have never asked how you are earning such riches. Why should we share your sins now?"

Even more frustrated, he asked his children.

"father, you have given birth to us. Obviously it is your duty to feed us. When we grow up we will look after you. But, why should we share the sins of your evil deeds?"

Thoroughly devastated, he went to his friends.

"Dear pal", one of the friends said sweetly, "you have helped us in need. By god, we shall also help you in need. Therefore forget the idea of sharing your sins with us!"

Now he realized the wealth, the power, the family, the influence and all that he thought he possessed were illusions only. And he had been slave to those illusions!

He returned to the Brahmin and fell at his feet, "Sir, you have opened my eyes. This moment I have decided to detach myself from every thing and meditate for inner peace."

After a long meditation, he became known as Maharishi Valmiki and wrote the epic Ramayana!

We know that friendship, family, worldly love, all these are not forever. When we die we go alone. But we fall for these illusions and become obsessive, possessive, jealous and over sentimental. When the wind of our desires blows our mind gets agitated and we become blind and "lose our head"! It won't be easy to calm it but we must find the way not to let ourselves spoil.

In what way?

By means of detachment that we must exercise from our youth. When a bad thought springs into our mind we must immediately replace it with a good one and, automatically the first one will disappear.

Many times we will see our attempts fail but we must persist. If we continue to struggle we will have, in the end, the satisfaction of reaching the tranquil.

Teaching Objective

Self analysis, strength of will.

Personality Test

- Do you never get upset as a result of some desire?
- When your desires are not satisfied do you get angry?
- With what interior instrument are you able to observe the mind and judge it?
- Have you ever noted that one desire calls another one?
- List useful desires and those that are useless.
- Are you capable of controlling your desire?

Questions

a. Who was Dashyu Ratnakar?
b. Why was he a sinner?

c. Why his family and friends were unwilling to share his sins?
d. Finally what did he realize?
e. Who is a real man?
1. He who lets himself be guided by his own desires?
2. He who controls his desires?

Carry out this Exercise

Explain how the love that you feel for a small child is more pure then the love you see in the cinema when a boy and a girl sing love songs running around the trees and dancing in beaches.

As you think you become.
This is PEACE 3.12

Teaching Value

To be in peace it is necessary to cultivate certain mental and physical attitudes to be coherent with ourselves.

Have you ever heard of the weight lifter who lifted a huge full-grown bull on his shoulder?

Well this is a legend from ancient Greek times of 'Milo' and the bull.

Milo was small boy who lived in Croton, Ancient Greece. You know the modern day Olympic games started during 2nd century A.D., i.e., 1900 years ago; and at that time they were called Olympiads.

Milo had just one dream to be an Olympic champion in wrestling. So determined he was that he worked out physical exercises and weight lifting all the time. Always he tried to find innovative ways to do the daily work outs.

One day their cow gave birth to a healthy calf. While watching the calf playing the boy had an idea, "why don't I lift this calf on my shoulders?" With some difficulty he could lift the calf. This next day again he lifted it on his shoulders. And he continued it for years without failing a single day.

Each day, the bull gained weight, and Milo lifted it atop his shoulders. By the time the bull reached maturity, Milo had gained enough strength to lift it in the Olympiad; and went on to victory in the Olympic arena.

All of us have to decide the path we follow from very young age and follow it without failing. This only will help us maintain peace throughout our life.

In which of the four situations would you prefer to find yourself? What type of person are you or would you like to be?

Behaviour is the index of our thoughts and it is impossible to lie. The truth always comes to surface when it refers to our personality. To be in peace it is necessary to cultivate certain mental and physical attitudes and to be coherent with ourselves.

Look at the pictures with two negative situations and two positive ones.

Do you avoid the blind man asking for help?

Do you hit the street dog just for fun?

These deal with the duties we have towards ourselves, our parents and old people. How would you behave?

To choose what we want to be it is indispensable to "look inside ourselves", get to know ourselves perfectly and thus decide what to do.

Do you water the plants regularly?

Do you leave seat to the elderly lady?

No one is so base as to desire or prefer to the person in the first two pictures. However not to become such we must learn to cultivate in ourselves the sense of values.

Only if we are coherent with ourselves and with our values will we be able to make useful and wise choices.

Teaching Objective

Interior riches, determination, altruism, interdependence between peace and duty.

Personality Test

- Do you think always before acting?
- Are your actions always in harmony with your intentions?
- In what way does your peace depend upon the choices you make?
- Do you prefer to maintain the friendship of a companion or to remain faithful to your convictions?
- Are you always in agreement with what your parents tell you?

- If not, do you explain them your viewpoint?
- What do you prefer to be?
- What have you done so far towards fulfilling your ambitions?

Questions

a. What did you learn from the story of Milo the Greek?
b. What determines your behaviour?
1. Good manners?
2. Knowledge?
3. The examples of others?
4. The mass media?
5. The company you keep?
6. The advice of adults?
c. To be able to respect others the following values are necessary: Generosity, ability, altruism, respect, patience, care. Indicate the reverse of these values.

Carry out this Exercise

How would you want to educate your children?

Desires have no end. Let's conquer it. This is the PEACE 3.13

Teaching Value

It is impossible to be at peace when we are not content with what we possess. The more our desires increase the more our peace diminishes: it is a question of inverse proportionality.

One day a disciple of Buddha asked him, "Sir, every day we preach about peace and happiness. So many people listen to us. Why then, there is so much of sorrow in this world?"

Buddha smiled, "I shall answer your question, but first do me a favour: when you go to the nearby township for alms ask everybody you meet what he wants."

The disciple did accordingly and returned in the evening. He bowed before him and asked the same question, "why there is so much sorrow in this world?"

Buddha replied, "Didn't you get the answer? Tell me what they said?"

"O Enlightened", replied the disciple, "I asked each and every person in the town. Somebody wants cows, another wants lots of gold and a house, somebody desires for a beautiful wife, someone wants son, somebody delicious food, then some other wants to go pilgrimage while another wants to be a king. The king wants to conquer his neighbouring kingdom whereas his minister wants to place his son in the king's court…."

Buddha interrupted, "tell me if anybody desired peace and happiness?"

The disciple now understood, "No! Not a single person wanted that! They think they will be happy automatically once their desires are fulfilled."

"Now you know," Buddha explained, "instead of seeking happiness and peace most of us seek pleasures in life, and lose our peace in doing so. That's why there is great sorrow in this world!"

Nothing has changed since. If we ask ourselves we also find our desires are limited to smalltime pleasures that have no end at all. The person who owns a bicycle desires for a motor bike; he who has a motor bike desires for a small car; the owner of a small car wants a big car; the owner of a big car thinks of a chauffer driven sedan whereas its owner thinks of a limousine. The owner of a limousine dreams of a private aero plane; and he who has a private plane desires for a Jumbo jet or a nuclear powered cruise….so on and so forth.

Have you ever thought you will be the happiest person when you own any of these or, for that matter, all of these? Well, the moment you acquire these, you'll look upon the man who has more, and you will be in great sorrow!

Desire is like a nettle rash. The more we scratch the more we like to scratch! And in this way we waste our lives over things that have no real meaning.

How do we find the peace and joy that lasts? Sacrifice and detachment are the fundamental elements for obtaining it.

Start by sacrificing something to make members of your family happy, or a friend or a companion. Their joy will transform your effort into your joy. Keeping on doing this day after day it will become ever more easy to renounce the superfluous and feel more serene.

Teaching Objective

Sacrifice or renunciation, control of the desires, will, generosity, great interior richness.

Personality Test

- Does having many things give you pleasure?
- Is what you have sufficient?
- What could you eliminate from your room?
- Do you feel comfortable when you keep everything for yourself?
- Will you give something of your own to a companion of yours who has less than you?
- When you have done this did you feel happier? Are you able to explain why?

Questions

a. Why did the disciple of Buddha found sorrow in this society?
b. When he asked everybody what was their reply?
c. What does being satisfied mean?
d. What makes you unhappy?
1. Possessing so many things?
2. Not sharing them with others?
3. Having few things?
e. On what does your happiness depend?
1. From the things you possess?
2. From the consideration you have for the things around you?
3. From the possibility to let others share in the things you possess?
4. From which you are missing?
f. Are you envious of your companions who possess more than you?

Carry out this Exercise

Explain why being satisfied is a virtue whereas greed is mental poverty. Give examples.

Love

Begin the Day with Love, continue it with love and finish it with love. This is LOVE 4.1

Teaching Value

The HEART has always been considered the center of the SPIRITUAL ACTIVITY of man. It is the seat of his sentiments and it is the motor that moves him. Love is like the blood that heart makes to circulate in the body. It nourishes us and gives vitality to our organs.

We are born from an act of love and we are able to survive only due to many acts of love that our parents perform daily.

We must never forget that all our life is an act of love.

But the king of Varanasi seemed to forget that. His story is there in the Jataka tales. Although a good king and

compassionate to his subjects, he spent a lot of time hunting for sport and killing numerous innocent animals and birds. With days passing the frequency of his hunting went on increasing; royal elephants crushed the small plants and animals, courtiers never spared any pregnant or baby animals. Particularly the deer population was the worst affected. Almost everyday they were hunted mercilessly.

In one of his previous lives Buddha had taken birth as a musk deer and lived in that jungle. Every day he helplessly watched his pals being killed with a heavy heart and tearful eyes. "Why there are so many killings? Human being is the supreme creation of the nature. If he is incapable of loving and protecting the inferior creations, what is the use being a man?" the deer would always think.

One day he gathered courage and went to meet the king. It was morning and the king was preparing himself for a grand hunting party. The best of his archers were there to accompany him. The drummers had already started pounding the drums.

The deer quietly passed through the royal garden hiding himself among the bushes. When he saw the king he went near him straightaway, the fragrance of his musk mesmerizing everybody.

With a polite voice he greeted the king.

The king stood speechless seeing this extraordinary deer that talked like an educated man and had a rare glow around him.

"O king! I am a subject of yours as I live in the jungle of your kingdom. Can I ask you some thing?" asked the deer, "Are you on a hunting trip?"

"W..W..Well, yes. But why do you ask?" replied the startled king.

"Sir, almost every day you and your courtiers go for hunting. Numerous animals have been victims of your pastime. There is sadness everywhere in the jungle. All the time the mothers and children cry for their dead pals. I just can't see their pathos. Therefore I have a request, please kill me and take out the invaluable musk from my inside. This will fetch you enough gold to fill your royal treasury. In return please promise me that the killing of those innocent animals will be stopped."

The king was spellbound. Here in front of him is standing an animal; who wishes to donate his life for others. Life, which everybody loves, and even the yogis and rishis do whatever they can to stay alive. A mere animal wishes to give his life for others!

He looked over the deer's body, "Look! You have such a beautiful body and rare invaluable musk. One gets such a rare gift after perhaps a million births! Don't you love your body; you wish to lose it just like that?"

The deer smiled, "Your highness is this body eternal? One day I will die and this beautiful body will become soil. And the love you are talking of is not love it's greed. Love is not selfish and never asks any thing in return.

I exist because I am being loved by nature, which provides me with light, green grass and water; I am being loved by my parents, they fed me and made me what I am today; not because of greed, but because of love.

Now my time has come. I must display that the love, which has been injected in me, has never failed me. If you accept my offer, I will be the happiest one because at least this body will serve a purpose today rather than being wasted away just like that!"

The king's eyes were wet. Today an animal told him what he could not understand throughout his life. The body that he possessed and took so much care would perish one day just like that! So far he has never displayed the love that was inside him.

He embraced the deer. That day onwards the king concentrated on displaying love. The killings were stopped. And his kingdom started shining with love and happiness!

In fact we must learn never to be afraid of demonstrating our love towards others: only by doing this that we bring alive human values, which are the only ones truly able to guarantee a serene and active existence.

To do this it is necessary to provide oneself with positive qualities such as sympathy, cleverness, humility, will and activeness; and get rid of the negative tendencies such as dislike, pride, willfulness, anger and laziness.

Teaching Objective

Self-analysis, understanding of our own value, sense of responsibility, justice, equality, fraternity, liberty.

Personality Test

- Do you always tell the truth?
- Do you always do the right actions?
- Do you love someone who hates you?
- Do you know how to be calm and patient in adversity?

- Do you know how to love every living thing, animals and plants?
- How much are the values developed in yourself?

Questions

a. Do you think hunting or killing some thing is entertainment?
b. Why were the animals in the jungle sad?
c. What prompted the musk deer to approach the king?
d. In what way he wanted to display his love?
e. What must we do to reawaken the values in ourselves?
f. Are you ready to make sacrifices to assert the importance of the human values?

Carry out this Exercise

Explain the five human values.

Love is not love until it shows itself as such. This is LOVE 4.2

Teaching Value

In life there are a thousand occasions for getting angry, but the real reasons are only two: an unsatisfied desire or wounded pride. Therefore life is a continuous struggle against our negative tendencies and victory over them signifies the purification of the heart.

LOVE is a SPIRITUAL ENERGY that in fact represents the essential morality and helps us in getting rid of the negative tendencies. We have well understood that love is not something to keep to ourselves but some thing we must give by helping, because in the first case it diminishes and in the second, it increases.

The virtues that compose this love are:

HAPPINESS is innate in he who is capable of love.

TOLERANCE is an expression of love which is within us and helps us to react in a quiet and intelligent way to situations which otherwise would be a disaster.

FRIENDSHIP is the purest expression of love. Who finds a friend finds a treasure.

KINDNESS shows itself always in him who is full of love for others.

SINCERITY dwells in the heart of him who knows the law: truth always comes to surface!

PARDON is the sentiment that shows itself when we love our neighbour and truly respect him.

COMPASSION is a lofty sentiment which we have if we find ourselves in contact with persons who, for various reasons are suffering and we feel ourselves bound to do some thing to lessen their suffering.

GENEROSITY belongs to he who has a noble spirit. It leads us to help those who are much weaker or less fortunate than we are.

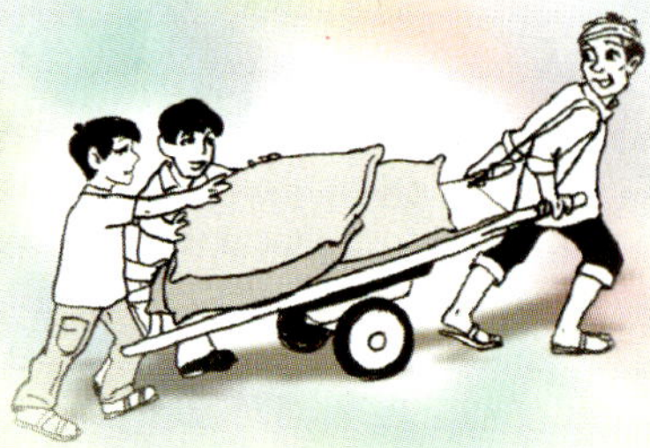

Finally, ALTRUISM, which is the apex of various components of love. It means to love without asking anything in return only because love is the expression of our true nature.

These are the virtues that are able to make us invincible in every struggle. Everyone possesses them and if he uses them he is destined to become an example for all the others.

Teaching Objective

Self analysis.

Personality Test

- When you love are you happy?
- Are you tolerant?
- Is it easy for you to pardon when you love?
- Does every thing seem more beautiful to you when you love? Why?
- Are you convinced that love is universal?
- Do the animals also love?
- Look for a synonym of kindness, of Divinity, of altruism and of understanding

Questions

a. What is a component?
b. What does love in action represent?
c. What do you call someone who keeps that does not belong to him?
d. Why do we say that love is a group of virtues?
e. Can friendship exist without love?
f. Do you know how to be loving with your companions?
g. Do you know how to smile and understand even when the others show themselves ill natured?

Carry out this Exercise

Explain how even a little gesture of love can heal great wounds.

Love in our life means passing from I to we. This is LOVE 4.3

Teaching Value

Let me tell you a story the story of Narcissus plant. Narcissus plant is just like an onion plant, but its flowers are very beautiful.

There is a famous Roman myth. A long time ago there lived a man called Narcissus. He was a very handsome man. You know those days there was no mirror. That's why Narcissus had no idea how handsome he was. However, when people looked at him with appreciation and admiration he felt proud.

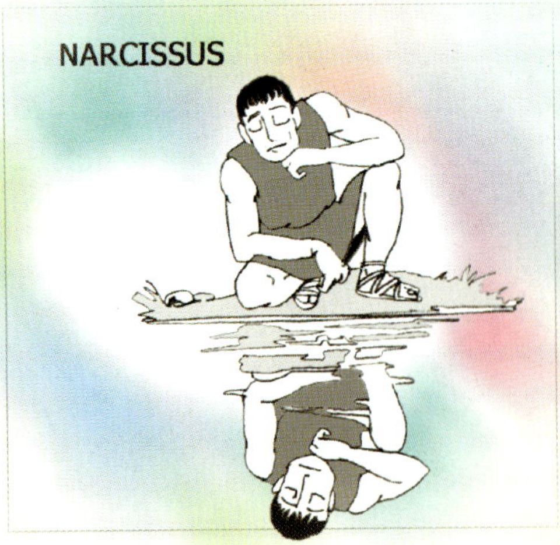

One day he was roaming in the jungle when he saw a small pond full of crystal clear water. There was nobody around and even the breeze was not blowing. The water was still just like a mirror.

When Narcissus went near it he could see his reflection. He was so handsome! Immediately he fell in love with his own reflection. "How wonderful! I must keep this image in my room," he said to himself and jumped into the water.

But the tragedy is that whenever he entered the pool, ripples formed and the reflection would disappear. He would search and search every inch of the pond but could not find his image. He would come back to the bank and sit silently. Slowly when the ripples disappear there was his reflection again, the object of his love. Again he would jump into the water.

The more he tried he became more obsessed and finally went mad and died on the bank. In his memory we have the plant Narcissus. It grows just by the side of the pond and goes on looking in.

What do we learn from the story? Love is not to love ourselves only. Love is not selfishness. If we indulged with ourselves only we become Narcissus and end up loving our own reflection.

The self-indulged person can no longer communicate with anybody. In return nobody cares for him. He is cut off from the world. But who is to blame?

As we all very well know, love is a treasure that multiplies itself when it is given to others and that diminishes when it is kept to ourselves. In hindi we say "Pyar baantne se barhta hai". Isn't that true?

Teaching Objective

Value of individual effort, from contraction to expansion.

Personality Test

- Do you feel happy if you are far away from others?
- Is it easy to live together with others?
- Are you indifferent to the suffering of others?
- What is solitude?
  1. Not to have anyone around?
  2. Not to be able to live with others?
  3. Not to love others?

4. To live only for ourselves?
5. Not to make sacrifices?

Questions

a. Have you ever noticed your reflection in the water?
b. What did Narcissus see in the water?
c. Why did he want his image?
d. If you were in place of Narcissus what would you do?
e. What does the story teach us?
f. What can make a man selfish?
g. Is it true that the selfish is alone even if in company?
h. How can a selfish person or egoist become an altruist?

Carry out this Exercise

Explain the phrase, "GIVING WE BECOME RICHER".

The man that is content will never be poor. The man that is never content will never be rich. This is LOVE 4.4

Teaching Value

Love is important, not money! He who is conscious of his own values and hence interior riches, will not be sad for the upsets and failures of life, but will accept every adversity with a happy heart.

The real poor man is he who, having material riches but not having developed in himself virtues and values, is always sad and unhappy.

Once a young sociologist visited a madhouse for his research work. It was a very posh madhouse, which only wealthy people could afford.

THE RICH

During his visits he noticed a woman patient in her fifties sitting in the middle of a busy corridor of the madhouse. She used to sit there routinely although it created problems for others. If the staff tried to force her out she would scream and hurt herself. Then she would return to the same spot and sit there sternly never talking to anybody.

Doctors thought her to be an extreme case and had no hope at all.

This young researcher decided to study her behaviour. He went there everyday and sat just in front of her. But there was no impact on the woman. She sat there as usual sternly looking at him as if he was a stone. The doctors and staff laughed at him for his foolishness. But he continued to sit in front of her without talking or approaching her.

A month went by without any result. Then one day he had some personal problem, so he could not visit her. That day the mad woman became restless to everybody's surprise and went near the window to look for him. That was a breakthrough! She had never recognised anybody since she was brought into the madhouse.

Next day when he came and greeted her she smiled at him. The researcher had achieved his goal. Within next few weeks he started to talk to her and together they strolled in the garden. She stopped sitting in the middle of the corridor. It was a miracle for the doctors!

The sociologist, who later became a professor of social psychology, puts his point very clearly: love and companionship can never be bought by money.

As in this case, the woman belonged to super rich class. She had every possible form of entertainment and pleasure. Why then she became mad? Just that she could not find love!

That's why she responded to an unknown person, who she thought had cared for her in spite of her madness. In contrast, her relatives and friends, who enjoyed numerous pleasures of her money, had now abandoned her.

Nature has every thing stored for us. We are gifted with a very powerful brain - to work, to create, to earn our livelihood; but certainly not to amass wealth just for greed. Riches and poverty are not dangerous until they produce greed.

He who is conscious of his own values, and hence of his interior riches, will not be sad for the upsets and failures of life, but will accept every adversity with a gay heart.

There is a flip side to it!

You must have seen people praying, "O God! Please give me more money."
Isn't it so funny? God has not created money; man has created it. Then tell me how would God know what it means. How will he understand what you are praying for?!!

Teaching Objective

Interior equilibrium, character, detachment.

Personality Test

- When you want something are you sad until you get it and when you possess it are you sad because you are afraid to lose it?
- How do you practice love that is in you:
  1. Towards friends?
  2. Towards your parents?
  3. Towards your teachers?
  4. Towards plants?
  5. Towards animals?
- Do you share your possessions with your friends/brothers/sisters?
- If not, why not? If yes, why?
- What is more important to you - interior riches or material wealth? Why?
- If some one offers you lot of wealth in exchange for your family and friends would you accept it?

Questions

a. Why did the researcher choose to study the mad woman's behaviour?
b. Did he succeed in befriending her?
c. Why did the woman become his friend?
d. Why do you think she went mad?
e. From what do you understand that one is poor and the other is rich:
  1. From their dress?
  2. From their behaviour?
f. What unites the rich man and the poor man?
g. What is true poverty?
h. What is true riches?
i. What are the signs of interior riches?
  1. Indifference?
  2. Detachment?
  3. A smile?

Carry out this Exercise

Love is important, not money! Explain it through your own experience or a story.

Do not do to others that which you would not want to be done to you. This is LOVE 4.5

Teaching Value

Look at the pictures first. The topic proposed is common enough in children as it is in adults.

To reply to the question will show clearly our nature, our intelligence, our degree of aggressiveness, our real character and disposition.

In the questions and the pictures that illustrate them, there exists an evident directive towards the right way to behave.

Egoism is to have and to forget being given, whereas **Altruism** is to give and to pardon.

This topic also illustrates the concept of love and how, in given circumstances, it must be demonstrated.

Do I return evil for evil?

Returning evil for evil received means putting ourselves on the same level as he who does the evil in the first place.

Do I walk away?

Why it is wrong to go away and not play anymore? Because in that way my companions will take me for a coward and will continue to persecute me by pulling my leg.

I am not doing them much of a good turn!

In the last case why is it **right to pretend nothing happened and continue to play**?

Because, by utilising a virtue of love, which is pardon, I have continued to play, even teaching them a lesson.

Note well that in the first two situations the behaviour has caused only fear, hate and scorn on the faces of the companions, whereas in the last case the lost harmony is re-found.

Man is a social animal, which means he can survive only if he knows how to live in the company of his fellows. For this it is always necessary to use the virtue of love, which is the only one capable of integrating us harmoniously in a group. He who pardons never loses. Even if, apparently, he seems to give in to avoid a squabble, in truth he is the winner - he is the one who knows how to keep everybody united over and above jealousy and suspicion.

Teaching Objective

Humility, pardon, love of our companions.

Personality Test

- If you are violent with someone how do you expect him to react to your violence?
- A true man is he who uses his fists or he who controls them?
- How do you react if someone insults you?
- Do you always succeed in forgetting the ill you have received?
- To be a "boss" is it more important to be strong or to be intelligent?

Questions

a. Why is it right or wrong to behave like the boy in the first picture?
b. Why is it right or wrong to behave like the boy in the second picture?
c. Why is it right or wrong to behave like the boy in the third picture?

Carry out this Exercise

Recount an incident where you created a trouble but were forgiven by your parents because they love you.

He who says he loves too much does not love enough. This is LOVE 4.6

Teaching Value

When we are children we love our parents, our brothers and sisters. This love is comparable to the light of a lamp that illuminates a room. When we get older and learn to love our friends and acquaintances this love is like the pale light of the moon, which does not illuminate completely. Is there a real merit in loving those who love us? That's why these two loves are not strong enough. The third type of love is comparable to the light of the sun that illuminates completely. This is the light of universal love, which makes no distinction and considers all men and women as brothers and sisters.

It would seem a difficult thing but if we practice a little at a time, we will become masters of this art of loving.

Have you ever heard of Namdev, one of the famous initiators of Bhakti movement? Well, Namdev was born in AD 1270. This is a tale from his childhood.

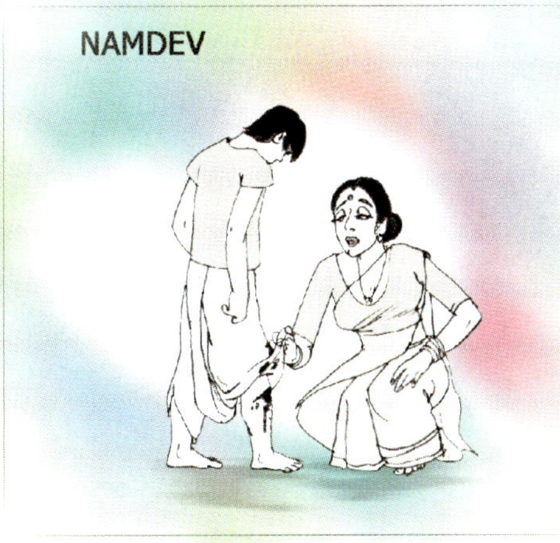

One day his mother noticed stains of blood on his dhoti.

"Namu! What happened?"

"Oh, nothing mother, I peeled off a little skin from my leg."

Mother lifted his dhoti and observed the bruised leg. With the skin a lot of flesh had come off. But Namdev was calm and smiling as if nothing had happened.

"But why did you do this foolishness?" she almost cried, "You could have lost your leg. And if the wound gets infected, we may have to get the leg amputated. Do you understand that?"

Namu looked at his concerned mother for a moment, "mother, then the trees should not be cut! In the morning you asked for the bark of the 'Palas' tree. While cutting it I wanted to know if the tree is feeling pain. That's why I peeled of my skin and flesh. It is so painful mother. Please never ask me to cut any tree again!"

This is universal love, which makes no distinction and considers all the living beings as his own self.

Don't you feel love for plants? Then consider this: There is a mango on the tree; it is outside. You eat it, you digest it; within a few hours it becomes part of you. It is in your bloodstream. After a few months part of it will move to your bones and a part of it will become your consciousness, your mind and your thinking. And then one day you will die and your body will be mixed up with the earth. Now the mango tree will take food from it.

Again...your body will feed the mango tree and again you will circulate in the sap of the tree, and you will become the leaf of the tree and the fruit of the tree!

So by loving it you are just loving none other then yourself!

Is it very difficult to love everybody? Not at all! If we practice a little at a time, we will become masters of this art of loving.

Let's start by making some effort to see the merits and not the defects of others. For example you do not like one of your schoolfellows because he is arrogant and never smiles! Well, try to analyse and understand the reasons for this behaviour; find in him the merits which he will certainly have, and you will see that in the end you will succeed in making him smile - you will start liking him.

Love is also an inevitable weapon. It is the only sentiment that can overcome the most impenetrable wall, armoured doors and the thickest bars. In front of the strength of love even the hardest hearts surrender! Never be afraid of love. In life, we can never love enough.

Teaching Objective

Strength of character, will, brotherhood.

Personality Test

- What type of love have you experimented up to date: the first, the second or the third?
- Do you believe all the living beings on earth are lovable?
- Do you see yourself capable of loving each and every living being?
- Do you make some effort to expand your love towards others, and who?
- Have you noticed some body you know loving everyone? (Mention one of his acts of love.)

Questions

a. Does the light of a lamp go beyond the walls of the house?
b. The moon illuminates:
   1. Outside?
   2. Inside?
   3. In both cases?
c. Does the light of the sun illuminate everything?
d. Why was Namdev's mother concerned for him?
e. Why did he peel off his skin?
f. What did he realize by doing it?
g. How is it possible to love every one?

Carry out this Exercise

Imagine yourself capable of loving everyone in the same way. What would happen in your life?

Love is Harmony.
This is LOVE 4.7

Teaching Value

Can we, in your view, find well-being, balance, and interior harmony by isolating ourselves from the world?

By refusing others and closing ourselves seeking to flee from responsibilities can we get to know ourselves and our merits and defects? No! It is impossible.

Harmony is the result of a combination of elements that differ from one another.

Don't you know how the first house was built? Well its a nice story; the story of two friends belonging to the Singpo tribes of North East India.

Long ago when there was no "civilization", two friends Kincha and Kindru lived in the beautiful forests of North East. Food was abundant. So they spent all their time playing, swimming and climbing trees. Life was a lot of fun!

Their only worry was the rains. The rainy days made them wretched. They longed for a dry place to hide from the rains. A shelter, which does not leak, would solve their problem. But they had no clue how to build it.

So they asked every animal around them. But none had the knowledge as well.

The elephant had gone to a far place. When he returned they asked him. He thought for a moment and laughed. "Come on boys, look at me", he showed them his legs. "What do you see? These four legs have kept my heavy body up. So you need at least four thick pillars like my legs. Then only can you mount a roof on them." And the elephant went for a mud bath.

That day Kincha and Kindru fetched four strong logs and planted them firmly on the ground. Now what? They did not know how to make a roof.

While they were pondering a snake was passing by. Kindru asked him.

He hissed, "You fools, look at me. I am light and thin and long. That is why I can travel from one tree to another with ease and eat bird eggs. Hi..hi..hi..sss. Why don't you collect thin and light logs to mount on the pillars?"

Immediately they went on to work. Within no time they had collected a bunch of thin but strong bamboos. But how to fix them?

Yet again they started their quest, "could somebody help us built a roof?" But none had any further knowledge. After a long search they met a she buffalo mourning over the skeletal remains of her dead husband. The animals had feasted on the carcass.

Kincha told to Kindru, "I have heard that buffaloes are intelligent. Why don't we ask her?" Kindru nodded in affirmation and they went on to ask her.

She looked at them with her gentle eyes. "Look at this skeleton" she said, "Do you see how all the bones connect to make a structure in which the flesh can grow? Similarly you need to place the cross poles closely so that they lean against each other. And then set a roof on it."

"But how to cover the roof?" they asked her. But she had no clue, so she drove them off and concentrated on her mourning.

They came back to put the poles in place and make the frame of the roof. Now everything has been done, but how to cover the frame so that it does not leak?

Their quest led them to the big river. Tired and exhausted they set on the bank to relax. A big-eyed fish was swimming in the clear waters. Kindru noticed it and showed it to Kincha, "may be she will help us."

So they requested the fish to stop by and solve their problem.

The fish smiled, "my friends, look at my scales, how they are arranged around my body. Go and gather plenty of leaves, mount them on the frame and arrange them against one another just like my scales. I assure you even a drop of water will never cross your roof!"

They followed the fish's advice and made a complete house! No more they had to suffer the rains.

What do we learn from this simple but profound story? Mutual respect, love and interdependence - in short Harmony; which has made the tribal survive with the nature since thousands of years.

On the contrary look at the modern civilization - our civilisation: what has it done? First we wiped out numerous plants and animals for our need and greed. And then we are on to wiping out our own fellows. Everyday we kill thousands.

We are scared of wild animals, thieves, robbers, abusers; we are scared of Sun and the rains and the air, the insects and pests, natural calamities and manmade calamities....we are scared of everybody!

Look around yourselves where this fear has led us? A lot of people keep guns for their protection...and yet a lot of them commit suicide by shooting themselves. Isn't it so ironical? Drugs and HIV/AIDS kill lot more than violence by others. See how much more our own pleasure seeking than any outward danger kills us!

On the top of that we have devised all kinds of weapons of mass destruction...all these within a span of only 200 years! And you never know one day a mad head of the state will declare war; and within minutes all the population will be wiped out from this earth!!

Which is the more intelligent way to live? Thousands of years with love and harmony, or a mere few hundred years without it?

And how can we find harmony if we are not loving and respecting others? It is only by mixing with "good company" that we will be able to find harmony in ourselves.

Teaching Objectives

The individual in relation to the group, the fight in the arena of existence, equilibrium, peace, comprehension.

Personality Test

- What does "your world" consist of?
- When do you feel really alone?
- When you are angry do you isolate yourself from others or do you remain with them?
- What do you feel:
  1. When you are alone in your home?
  2. When you are among the people?
  3. When you are in a garden?
  4. When it rains?
- Do you believe in harmony?

Questions

a. Who are Kincha and Kindru?
b. What made them wretched?
c. Which are the animals they learned from?
d. Think of any animal or bird and try to find out what have we learned from it.
e. Think of anybody you know and try to find out what have you learned from him or her.
f. What does harmony mean?
g. Which has led us to dangerous living, in harmony or by isolating ourselves?

Carry out this Exercise

Think of an alternative to war and discuss it with your friends.

Love We Are.
This is LOVE 4.8

Teaching Value

We come from love.

All right you can say we came into this earth because our parents love each other. But look beyond that, from where do they get the instinct to reproduce?

How come the plants got the seeds so as to multiply themselves? The flower has honey; the bee comes for it and carries the pollen grains on it's feet, and puts into another flower. That is how the plant reproduces itself. Which love is behind it?

What is the force that has created it all and fulfils all the needs of each and every living being on this earth? Do we pay the nature anything for the food it provides, the water we drink, the air we breathe and the land we live on? No!

See what I mean, it never asks anything in return and hence it is love - it expands…until infinite.

We are also love because we come from that truly inexhaustible spring of love. Therefore we must manifest it clearly in our life. We all love to watch bubbles which appear when raindrops fall on water. Don't we? How beautiful are they! Well, they also tell us about our life.

How do they form? Of course they pop out of water, live on water for a moment and disappear into it! Our life is also a bubble it appears out of the eternal energy that we call love, lives and disappears into it again. Just like the bubbles some of us have shorter life whereas others live a few moments more.

In other words, from love we come, love we are, to love we are going. We are, therefore, creatures destined to love.

Don't you realize it? Then I should tell you about Dr. Prakash Pandey.

He is a botanist by profession. In his college days he used to study with all kinds of plants, leaves and flowers. Almost everyday he bought a flower from the flower vender near his home and dissected it in his laboratory. Then he studied bit by bit under microscope.

He had gained significant knowledge of the flower - detailed up to the cells of it...until one day he fell in love with a girl!

The day when he first proposed to her, he went to the same flower vender to buy a flower. But that day it was not the same flower. He noticed how beautifully the colours have blended in the half opened petals, how its mild fragrance was intoxicating, and how the small water drops shining on it seemed precious pearls!

He never ever had the idea that flower is so beautiful and so intoxicating!

The same Dr. Prakash Panday was there and the same flower was there that he had been buying for years. But that day it was not a mere flower, but a priceless expression of beauty, of love; which Botany had never taught him.

That's what love is; it helps us realize the true meaning of things around us. Try and look at everything through the eyes of love, you will find love everywhere nothing else but love!

Teaching Objective

Tributes of love and taking the consciousness of our true nature.

Personality Test

- What does love signify?
  1. To give?
  2. To take?
  3. To think of others?
  4. To sacrifice yourself?
  5. To think of yourself?
- True love is a sentiment that exists within you:
  1. Can you taste it?
  2. Can you invent it?
  3. Can you destroy it?
  4. Can you touch it?
  5. Can you express it?
  6. Can you wound it?
  7. Can you increase it?
  8. Can you diminish it?
- Are you capable of loving?

Questions

a. Where does love come from?

b. Why do we say that we come from love, that we are love and that we are going to love?

c. Where do bubbles come from?

d. What properties do these bubbles have?

e. What is the profession of Dr. Prakash Pandey?

f. When did he discover that the flower is also an expression of love?

g. What objects symbolise love for you? Make a list of those.

Carry out this Exercise

Explain why you come from love, love you are and you are going to love.

Non-violence

The world is a single large family. This is Nonviolence 5.1

Teaching Value

Non-violence is synonymous with "Universal Love". He who believes in universal love considers all beings; animate or inanimate, as belonging to a single creative principle and hence to a single large family. Today, unquestionably, there exists a bit of confusion in the human family.

One day two champions of their own religion were having a debate in a train. It was quite a heated debate. Passengers had surrounded them. One of the debaters looked around and said aloud, "my religion is the most beautiful religion in this world. It teaches peaceful coexistence and UNIVERSAL BROTHERHOOD. Am I right?" He looked at the audience.

The crowd, who were the followers of the same religion, approved his point by nodding vigorously. The other debater was at a loss. He retorted, "I don't know what your religion says. But look at mine, and look at the philosophical strength of it. My religion is in fact the oldest advocate of love and BROTHERHOOD." The followers of his religion nodded with approval and pushed the others away from him.

The atmospheres was almost tense when a blind beggar crossed by. He sensed the dispute and interfered, "my dear fellows both of you say your respective religions preach BROTHERHOOD. But consider this suppose both of you had no religion at all. Then there would have been no difference between you two. That means you two would have been brothers all the same. Am I correct?"

Both the champions of religion and their supporters realized the fact and became silent.

Now tell me what do you think? Are we really different from one another? Only because our parents and leaders tell us to worship Ganesha or Allah; India or Israel…and so on? Suppose there was no religion; neither Sheela prayed 'Ram' nor Christina prayed 'Mother Mary', then what would have happened? And similarly what would have happened if India, America and South Africa all happened to be only one country?

We would have been just one family! Isn't it? Because you could not find difference between Sheela and Christina. And similarly you could not find difference among the people of three continents.

We all are same irrespective of where we live, what we eat or which language we speak.

You know what; it has been proved that the first modern human species lived in Africa. From there they migrated all over the world. Whatever colour our skins are, whatever language we speak, whatever lands we live on we are just one big family! It's just living for thousands of years in a particular place that has made us the way we look.

Then there arises a question should we demolish all our boundaries? But consider this our parents take good care of us. They feed us, fulfill all our needs and prevent us from doing wrong. Would we be looked after the same way were they grooming the children of the whole town? Of course not!

Similarly the boundaries have been made to take care of its citizens in a better way, not because they are a separate community or creed.

Therefore we are as human as the Africans or the Americans or the Japanese or the Eskimos.

In every family everyone has his own role and his own position, and so also in the world, as long as we do our duty everything goes well.

It is not like this when the parts get mixed up and duty is not performed. The family, at this point, enters into a crisis. Hence let us learn from our youth to consider first all our school as a little community as a family in which we seek to love and help each other reciprocally. The teacher must be able to consider the pupils as sons and daughters and make no difference between them. The pupils must have respect and honour for the teachers that they should consider also as teachers of life and living.

If we start like this we will not find it so difficult in the future to understand that the wide world is a single big family.

Teaching Objective

Self assertiveness, universal love and brotherhood, family values.

Personality Test

- What do you want to know about the person you first meet?
- Do you do your duty towards your family?
- What do you feel when you see a baby?
- Do you want to know its religion or race?
- Do you believe world is a single large family?

Questions

a. According to you what is a single creative principle that we belong to?
b. If there were no national boundaries, what would have happened to us?
C. What do you understand by single large family?
d. What were the two persons in the train fighting for?
e. According to them what do their respective religions advocate?
f. Do you quarrel with your siblings?
g. Do you fight with your parents?
h. What do you quarrel for in general?
i. Do you support them when somebody from outside quarrels with them?
j. Why do you think we should consider everybody in the world our brothers and sisters?

Carry out this Exercise

Suggest a method of your own to initiate the concept of universal brotherhood among your friends.

He who earns does not waste, he who wastes will never earn. This is Nonviolence 5.2

Teaching Value

It is necessary to learn the **four ways** in which violence can show itself, so that we can avoid violence in the course of our lives. Time, energy, money and food are the elements that are necessary for living and waste of these means waste of our lives.

We need to learn how to use our time well because time wasted is life wasted.

The energy at our disposal represents a "quantum" which we must distribute in an intelligent manner among our daily activities.

Money is necessary in order to measure the usefulness of things and not in order to be accumulated absurdly.

Finally, food is a precious thing and its waste brings hunger to someone else and hence is a grave sin.

If you look at the boy in the first picture he does not seem to be a violent boy, but he is.

How's this you will ask if there is no blood, if he's not kicking anybody, isn't carrying arms and seems completely innocent?

He is wasting his time. Seated quietly at his desk his mind is active but he is not listening at all what the teacher is trying to teach him.

Towards whom is he using violence? First of all against himself because he is losing the opportunity of learning which, probably, will not be repeated. Secondly, with regard to his teacher, who is speaking to the wall, by betraying the trust she had in him. Finally, in regard to his parents who imagine their children at school, engaged and intent to receive useful instruction for their future life.

In the second picture we do see a boy committing an act of violence. He is breaking his own money box to take the money saved. You will say that, after all, the money was his and he has not stolen it! Where then was the violence?

If the intention was to buy or to spend usefully his own savings the act is non-violent, but if, on the other hand, he wishes to satisfy useless or futile desires here there is violence. Violence in regard to whom? With regard to he who has earned that money with the sweat of his brow and his own work and with which he must maintain with dignity his standard of life and that of his family.

In the third we see a boy who keeps the lights on even though it is daytime, and is wasting precious electricity. To waste this energy is not only a violence in regard to our parents but also in regard to all those who have need of this energy.

The same reasoning is valid for the other sources of energy such as water and gas.

Lastly, here we see a girl who is wasting food without any regard at all for the person who has cooked it, nor in regard to who does not have it.

We have said before that Violence is an Attitude, an intention also if not made manifest. In our case the girl, by eating all the remains in her plate and thinking of children who dying of hunger performs an act of nonviolence. According to you is this good thought capable of arriving in Africa? Certainly!

Because thought has the speed of lightning and arrives everywhere we wish it to. But are the African children fed on thoughts?

No! They need food like us to fill their stomachs!

When we have good thought we are like little radios that send sounds over the ether which can be picked up at great distance. Someone will pick up our thought and will do that which we cannot do.

Teaching Objective

Respect for ourselves and for nature.

Personality Test

- Do you always follow your lessons with attention?
- What do you use your savings money for?
- Do you strive to finish the food on your plate?
- To whose advantage is it not to waste time, energy, money, food?

Questions

a. If you need something is it absolutely necessary to break your money box?
b. Why is waste of water an act of violence?
c. Why is wasting energy an act of violence?
d. Why is wasting food an act of violence?
e. Why are you told always to finish the food on your plate?

Carry out this Exercise

Make other examples of non-violence in our behavior.

Kindness, self-sacrifice and generosity are not the exclusive property of any single race or religion. This is Nonviolence 5.3

Teaching Value

An ample vision of life and of international relations (**Universalism**) on the basis of **sense of cooperation**, of **mutual responsibility and respect** and of **disinterested service** is the expression of non-violence which presupposes a spiritual conception of the world understood as a single large family.

Universalism means overcoming all the barriers that man has constructed in his path and considering every question from the point of view of its acceptability to all. Is it hard for you to understand?

Let's try to understand what those barriers are. The biggest barrier is greed. Greed has made man mean, he wants power and money.

Do you know the story of the goldsmith? Well…

Long ago there lived a poor man in a small village. His wife always coaxed and cursed him for being poor and idle. Then finally one day he decided to explore foreign land for work. You say oh, all the stories start like this. But wait, there is a twist.

One day while he was traveling across a jungle he felt thirsty. And he searched for a water source. Luckily he found a deserted well. When he peeped inside he was startled to see a tiger, a monkey, a snake and a man had fallen in the well and were awaiting help.

The tiger was the first to request. The poor man was scared initially but helped the tiger come out when he promised he would be grateful forever. Similarly he rescued the monkey and the snake and they were happy and asked him to visit their respective homes any time.

He then rescued the man. In fact the man rescued was a goldsmith from a neighbouring village. He also invited him to his home and wished him best of luck in his pursuit and went away.

The poor man reached a foreign land and earned a fortune. Then he decided to return home to his wife. He put all his money in a bag and started the return journey. When in the same jungle he visited the snake and the monkey and the tiger. They all were happy to see their savior and treated him as an honoured guest. The tiger even gave him some ornaments that he had collected from the hunters whom he had hunted instead.

Now our hero remembered the goldsmith who might help him selling the ornaments. The Goldsmith he was happy to see him. He treated him well and made him take rest.....Alas! The man showed him the valued ornaments.

Suddenly greed grabbed the mind of goldsmith he told him, "my friend don't you worry a bit. These will fetch very handsome amount. Please take rest and give me the ornaments so that I can go get those sold.

And what he did, he went straight to the king, "sir I suppose these ornaments belong to our dead prince. I have found the thief and murderer. In fact he is resting in my home. Please go catch him and condemn him with severe punishment"

This is where the greed for money and power played the trick with the goldsmith unlike the animals. He deceived the faith of his saviour - to get a berth in the king's court and a huge landed property as a gift in addition to the hard earned money of the poor man.

Of course in the end the poor man regained his status with help of his animal friends and the goldsmith received severe punishment.

The point here is the dark ambitions of our intellect that has made us separate; that's why the so-called leaders try to create a difference close to our language or religion or caste or the city or the state we live in or gender or income and so on.

Sense of cooperation means to feel the necessity of uniting all efforts to resolving all problems yet unsolved regarding poverty, hunger, epidemics, war and so on.

You ask, "but we are just small children. What can we do? How can we solve such big problems?" OK let me tell you another story no sir it isn't a story. A bunch of school kids actually let it happen.

One day teacher named Mrs. Kern tells her class about all the plants and animals being lost from the world's rain forests. The rain forests are being destroyed at the rate of 100 acres per minute. The children were horrified and asked Mrs. Kern, "Can you buy the rain forest in order to save the world?"

Mrs. Kern jokes with her friends about the children's idea and later finds out that it is possible to buy rain forest. An environmentalist begs, "Please buy mine." The children work to raise the money and someday hope to visit the rain forest they are saving for.

If children of all the schools unite guess what wonders can we achieve!

Do you **feel responsible** for the whole world? If I cannot answer for the actions of another that means I tacitly favour him.

Take the example of Pawan. Don't you know Pawan? How would you know? He was in my class when I was in 7th class.

In our school there were only two cricket bats. One of them was broken. And our seniors never gave the other one to us. One day three of my classmates decided to act, "Na rahega Baans, na bajegi Baansuri." They secretly stole the bat and broke its handle.

All of us the class fellows supported them because the seniors always ill treated us. When the teachers knew about the incident they called our class and asked who the culprit was. Nobody dared. But Pawan stood up and took the responsibility on himself. He was punished.

We all felt sorry for him. But he inspired us enough to let us collect money from all the class fellows and buy a new bat.

We got another benefit. Now the seniors could not take our bat. Rather they treated us well after that day because all the teachers praised our class.

It was Pawan's **sense of responsibility** that created a positive energy in my class and in my school as well.

Finally there is humility, basic virtue without which there is no progress nor respect, nor sense of **disinterested service**. Only this latter type of service can make non-violence grow within us.

Do you know once Gandhiji was traveling in a third class compartment; a co passenger spat on the floor in spite of Gandhiji's objection. He wiped it out with his own hands. The co passenger again spat. He again wiped out. When for the third time he did the same and gandhiji again wiped out his spit he was very much ashamed of himself. He requested gandhiji not to make his hands dirty and in return he promised not to spit again!

See how paradoxical it is! If we act on behalf of others in the end we act in the best way for ourselves.

Just think we all remember Gandhij and the world respects him, but does anybody know his co-passenger?!

Teaching Objective

Sense of sacrifice, and detachment, respect for nature, altruism.

Personality Test

- Nonviolence according to you consists in:
    1. Limiting ourselves to talking about equality between peoples?
    2. Dreaming of a world without wars?
    3. Seek to help those who suffer?
    4. To have understood the interdependence between all of us?
    5. Not to take into account the opinions of others?
    6. Tolerance of the cultures and traditions of the other peoples?
- Do you think you are nonviolent?
- Have you ever done anything disinterested for someone?
- Do you believe that, cooperating together, we can work better?
- Have you tried to construct something together with all your companions?
- Did you feel satisfied? Why?

Questions

a. Why did the poor man rescue the animals and the goldsmith?
b. Was it a disinterested service?
c. What was the reaction of all of them after they were rescued?
d. What made the goldsmith betray his rescuer?
e. Do you think you should or should not help such a person? If yes, why? If not, why not?
f. What happened in the end of the story?
g. What does universalism mean?
h. What in your opinion makes a man separate from one another?
i. Would you like to pass a holiday together with children from all countries?
j. Was Gandhiji's action a disinterested service?

Carry out this Exercise

Give an account of how will you explain an illiterate person we all are same irrespective of our different appearances.

An eye for an eye and a tooth for a tooth would make the world blind and without teeth. This is Nonviolence 5.4

Teaching Value

An eye for an eye and a tooth for a tooth would make the world blind and without teeth. How true! When we are under the influence of anger we forget it. The ego inside us always tries to inflict more harm to the person who has harmed us. Does it lead us anywhere except destruction?

I have read a mind-blowing story which I should tell you here.

There were two great soldiers. They had fought many battles together. They were friends and admirers of each other. Let's give them names Darsan Rai and Arjun Singh.

But today Darsan Rai wants vengeance; he wants to cut Arjun Singh into pieces and feed those to stray dogs! Arjun Singh is on the run and Darsan Rai has been following him since last three years! Yet the fire of vengeance is burning inside him like never before…

Darsan Rai had only two passions in life his sword and Radha, the most beautiful dancer of Vaisali.

They were very much in love. They had plans for marriage and children soon.

Then one day Arjun singh saw her dance in the king's court. He had never seen a court dance before. He watched her spellbound from start to finish. He was so charmed by her beauty that he straightaway went to her home.

When she told she loved his best friend, Arjun Singh was furious with jealousy and denial; took out his sword and sliced her head off in a wink…if not his then she would never be anybody's.

Today, after precisely three years and fifteen days, Darsan Rai is still following with vengeance the fugitive Arjun Singh like a dog village after village.

After two years of madness his family had caught hold of Darsan Rai, persuaded him to get married. He was married to a beautiful girl. But the flame of vengeance never diminished. After one month he again went on with his pursuit.

Two months back Darsan Rai found Arjun Singh and had a fierce fight. He had almost killed Arjun Singh, but he escaped with an injury on his forehead only.

Today Darsan Rai has found his hiding place. The informer has told him that Arjun Singh has been staying in this deserted cottage since last one month.

He rushes in yelling furiously, "Coward Arjun Singh. Come on, stand up..show me how manly you are." His sword shines in the darkness, his eyes blood red, mouth trembling with vengeance.

But Arjun Singh is already dead from the earlier injury and fatigue from continuous run.

Darsan Rai is thoroughly frustrated he could not slice his head with his own hands. He is furious with rage and unsatisfied vengeance. During such feats of madness a great saint intervenes. He advices him to forget and forgive the soul of Arjun Singh.

"But sir, my thirst will never be quenched in this lifetime's o ..oh…oh…" Darsan Rai starts crying desperately, "alas, nothing is left of my life!"

"Don't be a fool. You have your wife and family waiting for you. Go and embrace them. Everything will be alright."

"Never!" Screams Darsan Rai, "What will happen to my vow, how will I show my face to the people?"

The saint tries for a long time to console him but in vain. At last he tells him, "OK! If vengeance is your wish, then there is only one way. The spirit of Arjun Singh has been born again towards northwest direction. You can still take revenge by killing the child."

But how will I recognize him?"

"Oh! You remember you had injured him on the forehead. The new born has the same scar on his forehead."

Darsan Rai falls on the feet of the saint, "Sir you are like a god to me! Thank you so much" He kisses his foot and starts walking towards northwest immediately.

His village is there towards northwest. Darsan Rai decides to visit his home before further journey. After 21 days' journey when he reaches home, every body seems busy and happy. Guests have gathered and a celebration is going on. His father rushes to him, "Congratulations Son! You have become a father of a baby boy. We are celebrating the 21st day of his birth."

Forgetting his vengeance he runs to his wife. He hugs her dearly. Nearby his son is sleeping. With great love he picks up the bundle of joy to kiss on his forehead.. but..oh! What is this? He has a scar on his forehead..!

So, what is vengeance? It's nothing but harming our own. Perhaps Darsan Rai could have asked the king for justice. Doing an evil against an evil is nothing but fanning one's ego.

In the previous chapters we have discussed many times how everything on this earth is interrelated and born alike. Interdependence is the fundamental characteristic of the world in which we live.

If man realizes this he will work on the values of Truth, the Right Action, of Love, Peace and Nonviolence. The result will be sense of cooperation, respect, humanitarianism, and brotherhood between men.

Each man must do this and, by his own example, convince the others that they must come above their self-centeredness.

The great evils originate from man and in him we also find the great remedies. In this search man is not, however, alone. Over the centuries have appeared and appear still today great wise man who know and diffuse the profound truths that always accompany the evolution of man. We need to know how to listen to them and listen to ourselves, in the silence of our conscience, to be able to understand ourselves.

Teaching Objective

Cooperation and respect.

Personality Test

- How do you react to someone who wants to do you harm?
- Have you ever had an attitude of respect towards your teachers or your parents? Give an example.
- Have you never rebelled at the rebukes of your parents or your teachers?
- Do you accept poor marks?
- When you see someone in difficulty what do you do?

Questions

a. Why did Darsan Rai and Arjun Singh become enemies?
b. Why Arjun Singh was on the run?
c. What made Darsan Rai follow even after he was married?
d. What happened to Arjun Singh's soul after he was dead?
e. What would you do to your son if you were Darsan Rai?
f. Do you think Darsan Rai got a lesson?
g. Who should you listen to for understanding the profound truths of life?

Carry out this Exercise

Imagine a situation in where you reply to an attack with calm and without violence: express your sentiments felt during this experience which you have imagined.

Nonviolence is to see the unity of all humanity. This is Nonviolence 5.5.

Teaching Value

Humanity is like a mosaic of hearts in which every heart is important like every piece of the mosaic in order to complete the picture. This signifies that every individual, inserted in his own context, is extremely precious and indispensable.

If the heart functions badly, the whole body suffers as a consequence. Interdependence is the fundamental characteristic of the world in which we live. Look at the little world of your school or your home and you will understand the interdependence of each one of you in relation to the others.

I must tell you the story of Sweta. She loved a lot of things: she loved her parents, and her friends, and blue skies, and white clouds; but more than anything Sweta loved secrets. She loved to keep secrets from everyone. Keeping secrets made her very happy.

If her mother asked, "What did you do at school today?" Sweta would answer, "I can't tell you, mama; it's a secret."

In the evening she would be reading and when her father asked, "Beta, what are you reading?" Sweta would quickly hide the book and say, "Sorry Papa, it's a secret." And at school when her teacher asked the kids to write an essay on what they did on their summer vacation, Sweta wrote on hers, "Dear Teacher, I would love to tell you what I did on my summer vacation, but I can't; it's a secret."

Sweta had such fun with her secrets that she decided she would keep everything secret from everyone. So when her mother said, "What would you like for breakfast?" she said, "it's a secret."

Her mother looked a little confused and she said, "But how will I know what you want if you don't tell me?" Sweta smiled a mysterious smile and said nothing. So her mother gave her Upma, and even though Sweta would have rather Puri, keeping her secret made her so happy it almost made up for it.

And when her father said, "Beta, did you sleep well?" it made Sweta happy to answer, "It's a secret."

Her father also looked a little confused, then he said, "Do you feel O.K.?"

"It's a secret."

Her father looked worried, He felt her forehead. "Do you have a fever?"

"It's a secret."

"Do you need to see a doctor?"

"It's a secret."

Sweta's father went into the kitchen and whispered something to her mother.

At school when the teacher asked, "Sweta, what's 12 times 6?" Sweta said, "It's a secret."

And when she got sent to the principal's office and he said, "Sweta, how come you won't answer your teacher when she asks you a question?" Sweta said, "It's a secret."

The principal was very angry; she called Sweta's parents and they came up with a plan.

The next day Sweta woke up feeling very happy because her head was full of secrets.

She couldn't find her favorite dress in her closet. So she asked her mother, "Mama, where's my favorite dress?" And her mother said, I know where your dress is, but I can't tell you; it's a secret."

That made Sweta feel a little strange but she put on her second favorite dress feeling only a little less happy than she was before.

Her father was reading newspaper in the veranda. It was a nice sunny day, the sky was blue and some fluffy white clouds were floating here and there. "Papa, why is the sky blue, and the clouds are fluffy and white?"

And her father said, "Sweta beti I know the answer but I can't tell you; it's a secret." That made Sweta feel very strange.

At school she asked her teacher, "How do you spell Universalism?" and her teacher answered, "It's a secret."

When it was time for recess Sweta rushed over to her friends and said, "What are you going to play at recess?" but they looked at each other, and then looked at her and only said, "It's a secret."

Sweta started to feel sad. She asked her friends, "Well, what are you planning to do after school?" but they looked at each other and then looked at Sweta and only said, "It's a secret."

By that evening Sweta was feeling pretty miserable. She went up to her father where he was doing some work and said, "Papa, after you're done with your work, would you take me on a walk?" Her father put down his file and said, "It's a secret." Then he put his file up again and wouldn't say another word.

Sweta ran to her mother feeling very upset. "Mama," she asked, "What's going on? Why won't anyone tell me anything anymore?" But her mother just looked at her and said, "It's a secret."

That was too much for Sweta. She started to cry.

Then both her parents sat down besides her on her bed. Her father said, "Look, when you are keeping a secret you are doing it for your enjoyment only. You don't think about your loved ones. Now you know how bad it feels if nobody is cooperating with you anymore...."

Let's consider Sweta's case in a larger canvas. What happens if nobody is concerned about anybody? And nobody shares any thing with any body? How the society will survive?

Each one of us has a part which he or she must perform being a part of an organization that has a reason and purpose. Could we eliminate love and claim that humanity could still be defined humanity? When love is absent humanity is also absent and the heart becomes sick. No people, no nation and no race can do without loving the others.

Everyday you can perform an act of love: great gestures are not necessary, a smile is sufficient, a "good day" said to someone who is lonely, or help given to an unknown person. These are all acts which make someone just a little less lonely and less abandoned.

Teaching Objective

Humility, pardon, love of our companions.

Personality Test

- If you are violent with someone how do you expect him to react to your violence?
- A true man is he who uses his fists or he who controls them?
- How do you react if someone insults you?
- Do you always succeed in forgetting the ill you have received?
- To be a "boss" is it more important to be strong or to be intelligent?

Questions

a. Why do we say that humanity is the heart of the world?
b. What is the link that unites races and the people?
c. Why did Sweta feel miserable?
d. Do you like to keep secret? Why?
e. How would you feel if nobody shares any thing with you?
f. When you are together with others do you feel happy?
g. Are you always ready to welcome your companions in your home?
h. Do you know how to sacrifice your pleasure to aid one of your companions?

Carry out this Exercise

Explain the saying: "Humanity is a heart divided outside and united inside".

Who said… "Lord pardon them because they know not what they do!" This is Nonviolence 5.6

Teaching Value

The expression of nonviolence is above all illustrated by a compassionate love for all creatures. But non-violence does not mean unconditional pardon and the absence of punishment. Pardon, compassion and patience must demonstrate themselves in given circumstances and not unconditionally.

Let me give you one example:

Once a rich man was bored of his life and wanted some happiness.

He heard of a preacher who served people and helped them to find happiness with his wisdom and altruism.

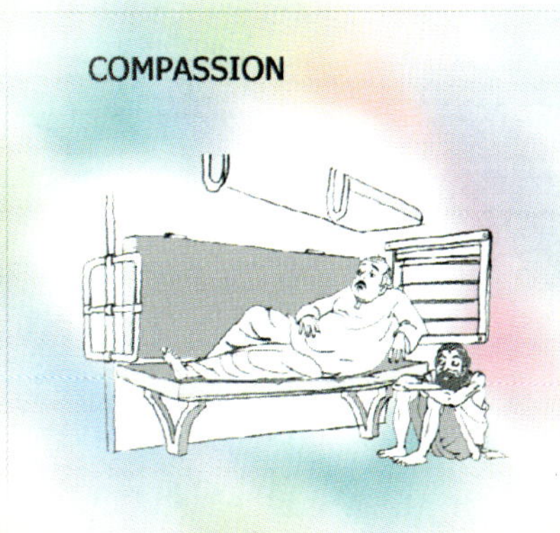

The preacher was supposed to give a discourse in a rally being organized in the nearby city.

The rich man decided to visit the preacher. A lot of people were also going to attend the rally. That's why there was unprecedented rush in the train. The rich man felt very uncomfortable among the dirty country folks. He sat on his berth aloof grumbling to himself.

The preacher started to give the sermon. People listened to him spellbound. The rich man also was mesmerized with his discourse; he had found a new joy in life.

His only regret was that he could have talked to the preacher one to one in the train and gained immense wisdom.

After the sermon was over the rich man reached the preacher with a great difficulty. He told him he was very sorry, as unknowingly he had ill-treated him.

The preacher told him, "I want to punish you for that."

"I would do whatever you want me to do"

"From now onwards respect everybody equally irrespective of his status, appearance or age. Because you never know among them there might be another me."

Many times punishment, indispensable for the correction of character defects, is a form of compassion. What good would punishment do to one who is not able to understand it from lack of intelligence?

As in the above case, the rich man could not have understood what was the use of the punishment before listening to the wisdom of the preacher.

Now, what would you do to him who does wrong because he lacks intelligence?
Pardon him! To know how to pardon is not only a great moral act, probably the greatest that man can perform because he must overcome his instinctive aggressiveness, but it is also a notable act of intelligence because it allows us to better understand our nature and that of others.

A man wearing rugged clothes asked him for a little space. He refused very rudely and stretched himself over the extra space.

The next day when the rich man reached the meeting place he was surprised to see the same man on the preacher's seat. He asked the people around. They confirmed he was thc preacher!

Teaching Objective

Love, compassion and pardon.

Personality Test

- Are you always conscious of the ill that you do?
- If your mother punishes you does it mean that she is violent?
- If you know that you have done wrong what would you expect?
- What difference is there between doing wrong knowingly and unknowingly?
- Are you able to pardon?
  1. At once?
  2. After you have got angry?
  3. After having been sulky for a long time?
- When do you pardon?
  1. Always?
  2. Only in certain cases? What cases?

Questions

a. Why did the rich man want to go to the preacher?
b. Why didn't he feel comfortable inside the train?
c. Who was the man wearing rugged cloth?
d. Why did the rich man asked the preacher for pardon?
e. Do you consider everybody around you equal?
f. Who is entitled to punishment?
  1. Who knows he has done wrong?
  2. Who does not know it?

Carry out this Exercise

Give an example of love, patience and pardon.

Nonviolence signifies not to say, not to look at, not to do and not to listen to evil. This is Nonviolence 5.7

Teaching Value

All of us know Gandhiji used to keep three toy monkeys. One had shut his mouth with his hands, another one kept his ears shut, and the third one kept his eyes shut. Here we have a fourth one sitting with them and has caught his hand. Now tell me what do they tell us?

Simple! They mean don't let your mouth speak ill of others, don't use the ears to hear harmful talk about others, don't use your eyes for looking at obscene, and finally don't do any thing that harms others.

The art of doing no harm to anyone, neither in thought, nor word nor deed is the essence of nonviolence.

Many people however interpret this in a superficial manner. They believe that it represents an invitation not to face up to the problems of life.

But "don't say", "don't listen", "don't see", and "don't do" are in no way passive attitudes. On the contrary they require great effort and sacrifice of ourselves to prevent our lower nature prevailing in front of temptation and provocation.

Its like I have two cats. One is white and the other one is black. Now it depends on me whom I am feeding. If I feed only the white one, it will become healthy and powerful; and always overpower the black one.

Similarly if we make conscious efforts to pursue the good, the good will overpower the evil and in the end we ourselves will become good human beings.

Making a habit of this type of behaviour requires, naturally, long and severe training which will be difficult for us to carry out on our own. It s therefore of the maximum importance to choose good masters, also by reading their books. These masters will know how to render our sacrifice more alive.

Teaching Objectives

Correct use of the organs of sight, hearing and speech.

Personality Test

- Have you ever tried covering up your mouth when you are about to say something unsuitable?
- Have you ever closed your eyes so as not to see something unsuitable?
- Do you always hold back your hand when you want to respond violently to someone who is provoking you?
- Do you listen only to good advice?
- Do you know how to be nonviolent?

Questions

a. What do the four monkeys tell us?
b. Why do we say that not speaking, not listening to and not looking at evil you don't hurt others and don't hurt yourself?
c. In what way can the word wound some one?
d. In what way can an instinctive reaction wound somebody?
e. In what way does listening to certain things wound?
f. What is the meaning of: "Silence is golden"?

Carry out this Exercise

Illustrate in what occasions you have behaved like the monkeys in the poster?

For Parents & Teachers

For Parents and Teachers

The aim of wisdom is liberty.
The aim of culture is perfection.
The aim of knowledge is love.
The aim of education is character.

The human values are the true richness of a society and are potentially present in the heart of every man and woman. The educative process is hence, the process that permits the perfection latent in man to express himself.

To my mind comes an example: two morons were hanging on a tall tree, sulking and clueless how to get out of it. One of them says, "I never listened to anyone's advice. Look where I have ended up." The other moron says, "But my dear I listened to everybody's advice!"

Therefore the children must be groomed in an atmosphere of controlled freedom. The values of Truth, the Right action, Peace, Love and Nonviolence are noble qualities that must be cultivated like flowers. Before, however, we cultivate any plant we must eliminate all the weeds that impede their growth. The hidden doubts and objections of parents themselves are the weed-bed to get rid of because they do not allow us to plant new plants or, in other words, to consolidate these values already innate in the child.

The future leaders of our country come out of schools and it is therefore extremely important that the teachers are up to doing their job.

The young people must be enabled to develop their personalities and prepare themselves to reach the higher stages of life.

What is important for this is the purity of heart of the teachers. If a student takes the wrong road it is not nearly so bad as if the teacher were to take the wrong road as in this latter case the whole class will suffer the consequences.

Only teachers who have humility can teach, give rise to good thoughts, inspire right action and instill in the young that devotion necessary to make them ideal citizens.

Final word:

Mulla Nasruddin lost his ring inside the room. He looked for it for sometime but couldn't find it. He left the room and started looking for it in the lawn.

His wife told him, "You have lost the ring inside the room. Why are you looking for it in the lawn?"

"The room is dark and it's bright here. My eyes can see better here." He replied.

We better start searching inside the room make some effort.

Young children can't understand the matters of value and wisdom is said for the sake of debate only. I am not commenting upon any body, but I'll definitely say that values I learnt from the age of 3 until the age of 15-16, had maximum impact upon me that I never had in my latter years.

- Surendranath Jauhar "Faquir"
(Chachaji Ki Madhur Kahanian and Prerak Prasang)

ANNEXURE—1

A Plea for Quality

We know that number or quantity is important, but we should not forget *Quality.* Let us produce quality children, give them good quality education, so that each one will be worth much more. In terms of food production, let us not only talk of producing rice and wheat, but let us produce more grapes, apples, fruit trees, vegetables, pulses, beans, milk and milk products and other nutritious food. This is quality food.

We talk of 105 Universities plus 10 Institutes deemed to be universities, several thousands of colleges and several hundred thousand of schools. It is good to spread education, learning and knowledge. But knowledge is power only when it helps some production and furthers right action. To know how to grow melons is of no value unless you grow them, or teach others by growing them. Let us have practical schools for agriculture technology, for trades and professions. Often agricultural schools and colleges have not enough or even any land where students can grow crops. Imagine, the diploma or degree which is supposed to indicate that you know how to do a particular work which becomes an end in itself and not the knowledge or experience that you get from this education.

The quality of men and material is important. We should build houses which last, roads which will not be easily washed away or dams which will not be silted up and become useless. We build dams, large canals and irrigation network without fully ensuring that every bit of the water stored or canalized is fully utilized. This is like buying a lot of bread when you are hungry, consuming what you need immediately and wasting the rest. This is happening with the irrigation canals in many places.

By concentrating on the quality, the implication is that each operation has to be given adequate emphasis. It is a matter of detail that one goes into that makes for quality. A nation or people are respected much more if there is quality. We have resources and brains. Let us muster the will to produce more of good quality things. At this stage of national development we need more and more quality and our past achievements show that we can do it.

Dr. M.L. Dewan
New Delhi

ANNEXURE—2

Teenagers: Self-Management and Health

Recently, there has been a lot of emphasis on continuing economic growth throughout the world. The government is keen to project India as a global technological and manufacturing hub as well as a knowledge economy. This status brings with it infinite possibilities in recruitment and training for people of all age groups. New frontiers in employment are now open to teenagers, and they can get a head start in their careers at an early age with the help of proper self-management. By following an ethical code of conduct right from childhood, they can achieve success and attain happiness.

What is Ethics?

Ethics is defined as morality or discipline in daily life. It is concerned with goodness of character, behaviour and virtuous conducts and knowledge of the difference between the right and wrong.

Good character and conduct can be achieved by following ethical codes like loving every one and performing actions with devotions and dedications without focusing on the fruits of actions.

This can be achieved by learning to do the following:

- Learn to think
- Learn to analyse
- Learn to give
- Learn to do
- Learn to love
- Learn to share
- Learn to care
- Learn to listen
- Learn to motivate

- Learn to encourage
- Learn to understand
- Learn to be flexible
- Learn to integrate and develop relationships
- Learn to be

Swami Vivekananda said, "Ethical values such as purity, patience and perseverance, consistency, concentration and cooperation give rise to success, but above all is Love". He also said that God's Love and compassion is unbounded. We must never say that we are weak, we must standup, be bold and strong and take the responsibility of our own destiny with ethical values.

Teenagers are excellent human resources. They can enhance and fully develop their potential by proper self-management, following ethical codes, and enlivening of their *prana* (energy), *ojas* (intelligence) and *tejas* (thinking). This will create a generation of perfect teenagers with dynamism and good health.

Dr. M.L. Dewan
New Delhi

ANNEXURE—3

Building Individual Character

Building **National Character,** a summation of individual characters (which has been deteriorating in the past years) and which is the key to all permanent improvements on the mental, material and spiritual planes, and which is to stimulate the development of the characters of all citizens of India, in particular children, who are responsible and not corruptible, to become the pillars of strength for a great nation. Citizens who will each carryout with efficiency and reliability the job or task that each one undertakes.

In context of children specific actions such as following will be stimulated

1. At home: Guidance of mothers and parents for bringing up the children properly and adequately and assisting in building their character from the beginning. Their task is to show how important it is to have a strong character, to be honest, to do one's share of work, to be truthful, to do one's civic duties, even to do voluntary work for national welfare and development.

2. In school: In studies, in games, and otherwise, the emphasis should be placed on strength to stand up to injustice, nepotism, unfairness, corruption etc. Movies, trips, camps, establishment and running of school garden plots and school forests, which are useful for practical work to gain an understanding of the importance of various relevant factors in character building should all be included wherever possible in school activities.

Talking of corruption, what are the theory, practice and economics of corruption? Generally speaking, corruption can be defined as the inappropriate use of power or influence which somebody has because of his position. This misuse can be and is usually for:

- (i) immediate private gains,
- (ii) political party, and
- (iii) pressure of one kind or another.

Some of its characteristics are:

(i) Those involved in corruption usually keep it secret,

(ii) There are laws in most countries against corruption. The lawmaker has decided that corruption is punishable, but often the borderline between proper and inappropriate action is not well defined, and

(iii) The borderline is often decided by custom. Custom varies from time to time and at place to place.

When the social machinery and existing value concepts of a society are destroyed, or when a whole nation has to suffer hardship and some even starvation while individual profiteers can live in abundance and luxury, it is difficult to suppress corruption. "It is hard for an empty sack to stand upright".

We can fight corruption by building individual character, promoting human values and simultaneously working on the economic prerequisites.

Source : *Agriculture & Rural Development: A Case Study on Dignity of Labour* by M.L. Dewan
The Human Values: A Task for All by Prof. M.R. Chilana & Dr. M.L. Dewan (2002), page 182

"Drops of Nectar "

Swami Chidanand Saraswati (Muniji),
Parmarth Niketan,
Rishikesh, Uttarakhand

Annex selected Abstracts for promoting Human Values

1. Peace - Internal and External

We talk constantly about peace - it is one of the most popular topics of world discussions today. Peace between nations, peace in our societies, peace in our schools, peace in our families, peace within ourselves. Yet, although billions of dollars and millions of hours are spent each year on think tanks, brainstorming sessions and international conferences, this much-desired peace continues to elude us.

How then to attain it ? What is the secret to finding this elusive treasure ? Let us achieve it. Peace - both inner and outer - are essential all else is meaningless.

2. Giving is Living

There is an old adage that says, "It is better to give than to receive". Yet how many of us actually live by this ? How many of us would give to another before taking for ourselves? It is not simple sacrifice. Sacrifice implies some level of suffering. It implies that one is forsaking something one wants out of duty to another. While there is a great deal of spiritual value in the lessons of sacrifice, this is not what I am talking about. For, in true giving, there is no suffering. One does not forsake anything. The giving itself becomes its own reward. People talk about cycles of life. For me, the true cycle is : *giving is living, living is learning, learning is knowing, knowing is growing, growing is giving and giving is living.* This is the true cycle of life.

3. Worship of the Mother

A mother is truly divine. It is from her womb we have come. Our life is a gift from her own; our nourishment flowed from her body. The love that sustains us, that embraces our soul, ceaselessly streams from her heart.

When I say your "mother" I mean many things. Of course I mean the actual mother who gave you birth. But, I also mean the divine Mother of all - the Goddess. In this Mother, we find not only our own mothers, but mothers everywhere. We find Mother Nature, Mother Earth, Mother Ganga.

4. The Danger of Anger

In life sometimes it is easy to get angry, easy to yell, easy to hit those we love. We assuage our own consciences by saying, "He made me mad," or, "She made me hit her." But whose hand is it really that hits ? Whose mouth is it really that hits? Whose mouth is it really that speaks harsh words ?

The goal in life should be like water - a stone falls in and only causes a ripple for a moment. The "hole" in the water caused even by a large boulder does not last for more than a few seconds. When we get hit - verbally, physically or emotionally - we should be like the water. We should be able to just let the ripples flow and, within a few moments, it should look as though nothing happened.

We must remember that our loved ones are like wood. Therefore, we must try to be very, very careful before we hammer holes into anyone, before we stab knives into anyone's heart.......if there are too many holes, the fence will fall.

5. Message of Budha

Service to others is the true message, the true teaching, the true wisdom of spirituality.

6. The Power of Love

We all have this power to transform not only ourselves, but others as well. Yet, do we use it ? Do we take the divine gift of love in our hearts and use it as much as possible, to help as many as we can ?

> Let us take to heart His divine message of
> "Love All, Hate None. Heal All, Hurt None."

God has given us a special ability to touch others with our smiles, to change a life with a simple warm embrace, to bring meaning to the lives of others by our love. We must use this divine gift and never let it go in vain.

Flowers blossom under the warm rays of the sun, and the flowers of our lives - our children, our families, and all those around us - will blossom only under the warm rays of our love.

If we learn how to love others, really truly love them, not for who we want them to be, but rather for who they are - for the perfect souls that God has created - then we have learned one of the greatest lessons of life.

7. Service to others is the Best Medicine

However, what else can we do, so many people ask, to really become aware of God - full of God consciousness - in our daily lives? We can serve His people! *Through service of the poorest of the poor we come closest to God.* It is easy to see the divine in holy people, easy to serve those who look pious, proper and beautiful. But, the spiritual challenges is to see the divine in all, to serve all - from the highest King to the sickest leper - as though they are manifestations of God.

Through this selfless service, we not only benefit those whom we are serving, but we also benefit ourselves immeasurably. Our hearts fill with joy, with peace and with love. Our lives become full of meaning.

8. Do your Duty

Usually in life, we know what our duties are. We know our responsibilities. We can see the "right" thing to do. This is especially true if we take quiet time to meditate, reflect and contemplate. Yet, too frequently we walk away from doing the "right" thing or from performing our duty due to the uncertainty of the result. We don't want to "waste our time" or "look like a fool". We neglect our responsibilities by saying, "It doesn't matter anyway." We shun our duties with words like, "Well, no one else is doing it, so why should I?"

This is not the way to live. We must realize that there is an enormous, infinite cosmic plan at work and we must all perform our allotted tasks to the best of our ability. Whether we actually succeed or fail in the venture should not be the biggest concern. True success comes not in a financial "win," but rather in the humble, tenacious, dedicated performance of our tasks.

9. Raise Yourself - Don't Erase Others

In life, in the rush to get ahead, in the rush to prove ourselves and make a name for ourselves, we frequently resort to criticizing, condemning and badmouthing others. In order to make ourselves look better, we put other people down. So many times we tell examples of the shortcomings of our colleagues so that we - in comparison - will appear better, or we criticize those with whom we are in competition.

However, this is not the way to get ahead or make a name for ourselves. Let us not try to diminish others in order to look good ourselves. That is like erasing the line to make it shorter, simply so we will look bigger in comparison. The way to get ahead in life should not be at the cost of others. Instead of bringing others down, let us raise ourselves up. Instead of cutting others, let us learn how to grow. Let us become long lines ourselves, rather than erasing others. If we focus on becoming as "long" as we can, then we will naturally shine above others.

10. How to walk on the Path of life

In our lives we frequently get frustrated and broken by feeling that others are blocking our way and thwarting our path. We blame their presence and their actions for our own failure. We explain to ourselves that we would have been able to succeed if only they had let us, if only they had moved out of the way for us. We try to push people and obstacles aside to clear a way for ourselves in life.

However, obstacles never stop coming. People who are jealous never stop trying to block our path. For how long can we try to move them aside ?How many obstacles, how many enemies can we try to push away? The answer is to simply find our own way, around them, between them. If they are blocking the path on the right, we walk on the left. If they are blocking the path on the left, we walk on the right.

ANNEXURE—5

Nurturing Human Values

"Human Values are the same in every religion and culture, while only symbols and customs differ. Only spirituality can nurture human values, can eliminate frustrations and bring contentment and happiness in life". —H.H. Sri Sri Ravi Shankar

Human Rights and Human Values

Human nature is cordiality, it is informal and friendly. And today in the world, this is what we have forgotten. We need to make a shift from living in a mechanical world to living in a cordial and informal world. This is the basis of all Human Values.

What are Human Values? Compassion, friendliness, cooperation, peace of mind, joy and a smile that lasts throughout our life. The sign of success is freedom. The sign of success is joy. The sign of success is a willingness to help and cooperate. Often in society, we find that crisis is based on identity. When a group is formed to specify only one certain identity, then somewhere along the line, a sense of belonging with the whole human race is lost.

Emphasis should first be placed on being a human being and then there will be peace in society and an understanding between people. We need to educate people to make them understand that one can be Jewish, Muslim, Hindu, Christian… but first and foremost we are a human being, entire mankind is a part of us and belongs to us, just as we belong to them. This is the understanding that needs to be created.

We need to create a sense of security from deep within, 'Human Values' means to develop that sense of security. This is another sign of success, compassion and security that dawns deep from within oneself.

It is also the responsibility of governments to make people more responsible and aware, and to feel a sense of belonging and be friendly to all those around them. Many a time, problems and issues can just be solved by friendly discussions. These are the values we need to bring to society.

The purpose of technology is to bring information and comfort to human beings. But when human values are ignored and neglected, technology brings fear and destruction. Spirituality is the technology of consciousness and the whole world is the play and display of consciousness.

We must not be silent about this anymore. The time has now come to speak about human values, to call the whole world to practice these principles.

Human rights is protecting others freedom, seeing the other person in yourself and yourself in the other person. Seeing that there really is no 'other'. Who violates human rights? Those who do not have human values. Instead of fighting for human rights—we need to tell others "Come on, wake up! See how human, how alike we all are!" This will shake them up, wake them up.

Human Values are understood to be attitudes, norms and behaviours which represent the highest expression of human life. They are common to all cultures and spiritual traditions, and include :

- A deep caring of all life;
- A responsible attitude towards the planet;
- Non-violence;
- Compassion of love;
- Friendliness and cooperation;
- Generosity and sharing;
- Integrity, honesty and sincerity;
- Moderation in one's activity;
- Service;
- Commitment and responsibility;
- Peace, contentment and enthusiasm.

The deterioration of Human Values in the modern world is the root cause of many of society's most serious problems.

Universal rights and peaceful co-existence cannot come about until hatred and intolerance are eradicated and a feeling of belonging develops among all people, irrespective of difference of races, religion, or ethnic background. Laws alone cannot be fully effective in achieving a peaceful and just society. A fundamental shift in attitudes and values is required. Violence will only cease when there is an authentic understanding of how precious every life is. Hatred will only cease when we feel that other are a part of us, when we feel a sense of belonging. Peace on the planet and universal rights cannot come about without restoring and nurturing Human Values.

Prisons, far from rehabilitating criminals, have become costly institutions that breed more crime, drug addiction and disease. We see pervasive family conflict and violence, high divorce rates, children increasingly raised in poverty. We see alarming rates of suicide among the young, widespread use of drugs, teen pregnancies, and violent crimes perpetrated by children and youth. We see school children with no sense of belonging, and racial violence in schools. We see commercial exploitation of human life, including child labour, child pornography, and trafficking in women. Women continue to be disempowered in most countries of the world.

There is a critical need to nurture an understanding of how precious each life is and the importance of developing the full potential of each individual. An attitude of friendliness and co-operation needs to be cultivated, as well as a sense of belonging and oneness among all people.

The survival of the planet itself depends on the development of "eco-friendly" attitudes and habits. Even sustainable development is rooted in the resurgence of Human Values.

Health concerns are also directly linked to the deterioration of Human Values. As our value systems break down, a deep sense of insecurity develops resulting in increased levels of anxiety, stress and tension.

The International Association for Human Values was founded by His Holiness Sri Sri Ravi Shankar to address the urgent need in the world today to nurture and re-establish Human Values in Society.

ANNEXURE – 6

AFTERWORD

TRUE EDUCATION IN HUMAN VALUES IS A LIFELONG OPERATION

My percipient Pilgrimage in the realm of 'HUMAN VALUES', began in early fifties of the 20th century when I joined as an untrained teacher in a village school of Ferozepore district in Panjab. This period of less than two months, when I was waiting for the result of my Intermediate Examination to be announced, proved determinative in my decision to spend my professional life in teaching and learning. Before finalizing my resolve, I considered it obligatory to seek permission from my revered father, who had dreamt of seeing me as a lawyer so that I could help him in winning his land disputes and helping others to fight against injustice. I felt that his faith in God and his life being full of compassion, charity and ethical principles will surely accord me his kind approval. As I spoke to him about this, I was amazed and amused to observe his face so radiant, luminous and effulgent. Spontaneously descended the words from his blessed lips, "Education should make people good and I will be happy to see you doing this noble job. But along with the bookish knowledge, you should also teach `Dharma' the righteous conduct".

So following this route of educating myself in EDUCATION, I attended seven years of residential courses, four in India and three abroad, organized by UNESCO and Commonwealth Institutions. My last formal study was in Birmingham University during 1976-77. Throughout my professional life and post-retirement period, the focus was on Human Values for my students and others with whom I came into contact with but more so for myself. In this process my concepts to deal with the subject have changed from *Moral Education* to *Ethical Instructions,* to *Value Education,* to *Value Orientation* and to *Value Creation.* At present, I stand for "Value Appropriation", which signifies unique taste of the invaluable fruit of `Human Values' based on my earlier experiences, I look at the true nature of man, the `WHOLE MAN', not divided in anyway, the true "GLOBAL CITIZEN" who could boast of , `VASUDHAEV KUTUBKAM—Global Society,' "the whole world is my home". His concern will be not only the evolution of man, but to be also concerned with all creatures of the universe, the plant world, ecology, environment, peace, human rights, Art and Science of living, spirituality, poverty and corruption, in short, every aspect dealing with life within and outside.

During this period of more than half a century I interacted with students of all ages, pre-primary to post-doctoral students, adults, army officers and jawans, employees in different government or non-government institutions, employees in business houses and NGOs. Human Values were the focus in all directions, its challenge, need and basis, sources, processes, difficulties, evaluation, special characteristics, cultural heritage, secular view, spiritual base, scientific influences, identification of values, present concerns in society and values and roles of different institutions research, planning and integration with related institutions.

As the opportunities were offered I studied philosophical basis and operational approaches of many prominent institutions. Some of these were publicized such as: Value Based Education of Sri Sathya Sai Baba, Rama Krishna Institute of Moral and Spiritual Education, Dayalbagh Institute of Radha Swamies, Banasthali Vidya Peeth, Krishna Murthy's Rishi Valley School, Brahm Kumaris' Ishwariya Vishwa Vidyalaya, Gurbani and Living Ethics of Nicholas Roerich. A summer course in Human Values, Yoga and Value Education, Swami Vivekanand Yoga Anusandhan, School of Practical Philosophy, Buddhist Value, Jainism and Art and Science of Living for college students, as visualized by P.G Institute of Innovatory Education and Service (PGIIES). Further studies are being made on, Islamic and Christian values, Arya Samaj, Anand Marg, Soka Gakkai International and School of Practical Philosophy. Invitations have been received from some institutions to help them identify their directions to promote value education programme. The writer enriches himself by assisting such institutions and knowing as well as interpreting their Value System.

The writer continued writing about his findings and personal experiences in Human Values apart from the published materials including in "The Human Values : A Task for All, brought out jointly with Dr. M.L. Dewan; my prominent books, brochures, monographs, pamphlets and manuals include, Value Orientation of Education : Pioneering Indian Experiments; `Manviya Mulyon Ka Shikshan - EK Gambhir Samasya: Kaise Nipetan', `Daily Appointment with Yourself', `A Value Structure Towards a Sustainable Society', 'Vedic Philosophy of Education and Himalayan Eco System', `Role of Schools and Developed India Vision', `Teachers must Grow and Glow', The Indian Teacher of our Times, In-service Education of Elementary Teachers and Value Education for Human Rights. Among the significant aspects of Human Value being the concern of educational institutions and society at large; brief write-ups have been prepared for the Criteria to select value content, direct and indirect methodologies, Role of ICONS and Role Models, Place and utilization of text books, evaluation of value education programmes involvement of parents, Role of mass Media, Preparation of Resource

Materials and Preparation of Teachers for Value Education as Critic, Appreciator, Implementer, Crusader and Researchers. In addition to the above many opportunities for lectures, discussions and discoveries in India and abroad, covered several topics. Some prominent ones included `Yoga and Value Orientation of Education', Yoga and School curriculum for Moral Education, Value-Orientation of B.S.F. Schools, "Value Orientation and Role of University Education Department in South Africa", `Values for Empowerment of Teachers', `Value Education - A Conceptual Framework', `Crisis of Secular Values and how to build up secular values, problems of Indian Environment and its Impact on Internal Values, Science and Spirituality. Responsible Resource Utilization (Human and Natural) A Media Consortium Positively to transform world Attitudes, Value Education for Better Society. These and many more issues were covered in different types of institutions including University Departments, Colleges, Schools, Internal Security Academy, Army Officers and Army Schools as well as HRD promoters in companies and industrial houses.

My placement as visiting Professor in the Faculty of Educatio in Rand Africaans University, Johannesburg, South Africa in 1995-96 was a wonderful chance to get positive reaffirmation, from the distinguished student and enlightened faculty members in my beliefs and convictions about different dimensions of implementing value education programmes in schools, colleges and society at large. Talks to students of Yoga Research Centre in South Korea helped immensely in delving deep in finding out the relevance of Rishi Patanjali's basic tenets of `Yamas' and `Niyamas' in developing Values. But my involvement as consultant in the School of Practical Philosophy was a unique time in 1995-96 to go to the vital roots of Values which help in full blossoming of one's personality. This is a unique experiment in the merging of eastern and western values. The credit of this vision goes to Mr. Leon MacLaren who founded the School of Economic Science in London in 1937 to teach the Values and Principles of truth and justice. He was trying his best to get wisdom from all over the world. In 1965, he travelled to India and met His Holiness, Shri Shantanand Saraswati, The Shankaracharya of the North. The conversations resulted in accepting the Shankaracharaya as the living authority for expounding the eternal wisdom of the great scriptures. Three fundamental questions arose to be the beginning of the search for the Absolute Truth, the highest value which is essentially the most significant for work in `Human Values'. The other values will be automatically accepted if the Truth is understood properly. In respect of the most significant goal of knowing the Truth, three fundamental questions emerged to be vital. These are : What is Creation?, Who is the creator? and What is any Relationship to them? The School of Practical Philosophy (SPS), as the present designation of the institution signifies, focuses on bringing out the importance and relevance of knowledge in the present context. They help the students to find out that if you look at anything seriously, you will find that it is nothing but the manifestation of the same consciousness, beliefs and truth, i.e `Satchidanand'.

The SPS, in this way brought, to absorb the three important values of understanding the `Truth', 'Expansion of Consciousness', and Being in the Bliss. Thus the whole task for a human being is to manifest this trio of related values. Manifestation means becoming obvious. Their conclusion is so impressive, "All things are made of Him; and without Him was not anything made. In Him was life; and the life was the light of man". The School (SPS) has been for me an ideal institution to further go deep in the three Values, follow the methodologies evolved by them to reach the goal of life. Continuing to do further research, I found the openness of P.G. Institute (P.G.I.I.E.S), very useful to dig deeper and deeper in Human Values. The process is enjoyable and bringing to me unique joy, satisfaction and bliss. The Institute is unique in being secular and all comprehensive to have the base of Teaching, Research, Development and Extension.

As evolution and progressive growth and development in my professional life and personal life is taking place, my faith in Human Values is increasing. I look at myself as well as any other person from the view point of my his/her values. My interview published in *The Times of India* was aptly entitled `GROWING UP WITH VALUES'. All actions are based on one's Value And one's Values are what one considers to be most important. If one likes to know onself, the right approach is to examine one's Values. Understanding one's Values helps to live a valued life. Above all, one must realize that the human values are at the top of all other aspects of man. They show the way to be good, better and best and even better than the best. If one does not start on this path, the result will be disastrous, nay catastrophic and ruinous. It will be much more dangerous for such a man if he gets authority. The title of another of my interviews published in *The Times of India,* New India was captioned `POWER WITHOUT GOODNESS'. The interview brought an apt quotation, `There is only one thing worse than the devil and that is the educated devil ?' He showed his complete agreement with my views that the foundation of right education is `Human Values'. Likewise, I view every happening in life from the point of view values it has emanated from. But it must be recorded that I don't judge whether the person or happening is right or wrong. In fact, whatever I hear or see, I say 'This is Right', 'You are Right', 'Whatever one speaks is right', because of the angle in which one is placed. In fact, every happening brings a feeling of wonder in me. Living and wondering has been my cherished pastime. As the time unfolds, I watch and wonder at every happening. It is like mystery revealed, though sometimes not understood immediately as to why it happened like that. Both situations help me to understand myself and my values. Readers may easily draw a conclusion from the above that I look at everything as it helps me in development and understanding of human values.

So coming to the elaboration of `Afterword', this after-thought emerging with understanding of what in stated in the publication by Dr. M.L. Dewan, Ashok Kini and Pradeep Nayak. This publication is an adaptation of the original book by Antonio and

Sylvi Craxi, published by *PERSONA*. I met them in Prasanthi Nilayam in Sri Sathya Sai Institute of Higher Learning. I was officially deputed to study important features of their value- based education. Both Antonio and Sylvi were impressed with the report I submitted. We discussed different aspects of how I perceived the system and made recommendations for experimentation in other institutions of the country. Their main concern was to spread the gospel of Values to the Western people. They were searching for the approaches to educate the Europeans. Thus the five-fold system of Values of Sri Sathya Sai is taken by them, but the illustrations and stories are presented by them on keeping in mind the western learners. On my later visits to Prasanthi Nilayam, they gave me a copy of their publication, "The Human Values - A Voyage from "I to We". Dr. M.L. Dewan, who is basically a soil scientist and worked with FAO for more than three decades, saw the book with me and liked the book and was impressed with the presentations and proposed to me to readapt the ideas for Indian mind. To me it looked like raw material from India, going to Europe and returning to India after the process. The idea was interesting, but I could not collaborate primarily because I have been busy in writing and researching on other Indian and foreign systems of Man-Making. I felt that my efforts to talk on other Indian sources like Gurbani, Rama Krishna, Vivekanand, Nicholas Roerich, Art and of Innovatory Science of Living in PG Institute Education and service Patanjali is Yoga and Veda's Soka Gakai will be more worthwhile. Any my efforts have been blessed to bring to me an inner solace and deeper understanding of myself, the world and the supreme. I noticed with wonder that Pradeep Nayak, who is a Mathematician and an Animation Film-maker, joined M.L. Dewan along with Army officer Colonel Ashok Kini. Trio have a common link of `Love for Himalayas', so we have this publication. Since I like all types of interpretations on Value Education, I must admit my inability to commend or condemn the contents and methodology. But I do want to reiterate that original is from Sri Sathya Sai, adaptation of which is the book of Craxies and readaptation is given by Madan Dewan, Ashok Kini and Pradeep Nayak. My concern is `HUMAN VALUES'. I may also call my write up as `After All' because these two words are uncontroversial, genuine, pure and the ultimate. They include `Innergrwoth' and `outergrowth'. Readers may like to think over the two process and contents of the publication. Madan may take this as `After-crop' with his background of agriculture. This may also be like `Aftermost'. Truly, this `Afterpiece' and `Postlude'. Indicates what should happen if these words are put at the end of the book. The readers may like to go back to the re-reading of the book and seeing the new meaning of each word. It will be like 'After-life', subsequent reflection, and `After-wit'. It may also turn into later or too late meditations. To me, every word appears as `AKSHAR BRAHAM'? To facilitate this happening inside one is self, it is important to be acquainted with myriad dimensions of Human Values. This will help in enjoying the re-reading of the publications and seeing its significance in the evolution of human personality.

The first and foremost point is that the reader should be convinced that human values are the true basis for one's best possible evolution. Thus one must start reading any book on `Human Values, with atleast the hypothesis that the prerequisite, to be a true human being, is to know, to understand and to adopt appropriate value system. This will help in proceeding further and gain the maximum. Reading Annexure I may prompt to improve the quality of individual and collective life and the readers may rise to work for that. Annexure 2 mentions fourteen directions to learn. One may identify many more such as learning to wonder, learning to love, learning to transcend, learning to ascend and learning to merge with `Supreme Bliss'. There are innumerable other stations in the journey of life where one may like to stop and stay to grow and know. Likewise, Annexure 2 & 4 indicate directions for building individual character, which should be accepted as the FOUNDATION for the future of MANKIND.

The Preface opens with the promise of how `REVEALATIONS' can happen, the story of a Rabbi and Hitler is a good illustration. There is also an inkling of `Inside world,' five qualities for human triumph and nine `Rasas' as juices of life. One may discover many other wonders of the `Inside World'. This book draws heavily from experiences of Antonio and Sylvie Craxi who learnt from Sri Sathya Sai Baba, the Indian Scriptures and many other sources of `Wisdom'. Fables and stories make the reading light and interesting. Each of the five Values is divided into sub-values and includes its teaching go to objective, personality test, questions and exercise. Readers may like to refer to the original book of Craxies as also many other books of Sri Sathya Sai Institute of Higher Learning. The writer has no doubt about the success of one's Voyage from I to "We". But let us think of `what will be thereafter?'

Naturally, it will be the joy of living as `We All Together'. There will be no narrow divisions of caste, creed, colour, sizes, beliefs, tenets, dogmas doctrines or any other system. All will go deep into `Human Values'. There will be deep yearning to Love, Loving to learn and Learning to live in harmony. There will be peace to other inside and outside. Non-violence will be role of Law with the righteous conduct. The life will be joyous, satisfying and all in grace, elegance and excellence. But another voyage has to start again. This time from `We to I'? But this 'I will be a different `I'?' more beautiful journey to the `Highest Bliss'. The yearning will be very deep and intense. One will live with wonder. While discovering the wonder, one will be silent and `JUST BE'? Then one will aspire to even TRANSCEND the `BE' situation. As one learns to transcend, ASCENDANCE will take place. This will lead to `Merger' in Bliss. And it will be Bliss in Bliss. This way, True Education in Human Values will be a successful Life-Long Operation. Doctor, `Heal Thyself First'. I am already at that - you are welcome to join. Finally, thanks to Faith Foundation, who made this book in its form today.

Dr. (Prof.) Mulk Raj Chilana
President,
Servitors Association for Value Education

ANNEXURE—7

Begin the Change

Today's society is running towards material contentment and in doing so, it has started loosing the human values. Too much effort to make money is not good as we are imparting wrong teachings to our children. It is high time that we wake up to these realities and begin to change the order of our life of our society. What is needed is regeneration of human values and more universal approach to life.

We live in a wonderful universe in which everyone and everything gives. The trees give. The rivers give. The earth gives. The sun, the moon and the stars give. However, alas, man is an exception—he is always anxious to receive, to grab, amass and hoard and not to share. This gives rise to discord and conflict in the society. Moral and ethical values are forgotten. Corruption, violence and all negative and destructive tendencies have gained an upper hand in society. In such a situation, **well-meaning individuals have to sit up and act to arrest this trend and bring about a total change.** If the society is to be saved from these degenerate tendencies, immediate steps should be taken to give thrust to **Value Based Education (VBE)** that would help build up character through moral and ethical values as distinguished from materialistic and selfish values, because our hope lies in the proper upbringing of the young.

Educational institutions play the most crucial role in imparting moral education to children. Let us plant the saplings of character building, and water them with a moral and ethical life in the garden of educational institutions. Character is even more important than vigour of body and keenness of intellect. It is the soil on which all must grow. If that is defective, nothing can come to fruition. Men must be faithful to their word, respect mutual obligations and be kind to one another and place the welfare of others above personal gains. Otherwise, the community as a whole cannot progress and the nation cannot march onwards, whatever be our levels of learning and the percentage of literacy in our population. We want that education by which character is formed, strength of mind is increased, heart is mellowed, intellect is expanded, and one acquires an integrated personality.

Schools should be centres of culture. Imparting education to develop the intellect. Educational institutions must aim at improving the quality of life and the standard of living of an individual. The former draws its sustenance from spiritual, moral and ethical values while the latter from secular subjects. Education, to be effective, requires the cohesive involvement of parents, teachers and students.

Text books or the school education should become a medium for boys and girls to learn what is right and what is wrong in life. Education should not take them farther and farther away from their fellow beings and confine them in narrow circles of their own comfort and advancement. It should enable them to understand and appreciate their rich heritage. They should become aware of their duty to their fellowmen and the country, in a spirit of extending the frontiers of their hearts and widening their family circle to gradually embrace the whole universe. Just as a bird needs two wings in order to fly in the sky, we human being needs human values in both material and spiritual aspects to life to make our spirit fly as an enlightened soul.

I am indebted to Swami Nithyananda Ashram and Swami Ramdas & Mother's Anandashram in Kanhangad which is promoting value based education (VBE) to build character in children through spiritual, moral and ethical values, for giving me inspiration to work for human values in the society. And I am also indebted to Dr. APJ Abdul Kalam, former President of India, who made me understand the necessity to revive the human values in India and gave me master mantra "If God is with us, who can be against us" and asked me to spread spritual connectivity in the society.

Peaceful be heaven, peaceful the earth,
Peaceful the broad space between.
Peaceful be for us the running waters,
Peaceful the plants and herbs!
Peaceful be all the Devas, Peaceful be the Brahman,
Peaceful be the entire universe,
May peace and only peace prevail,
And may that peace come unto me. Aum Peace, Peace, Peace.
Aum Peace, Peace, Peace.

Jai Jawan, Jai Kisan, Jai Vigyan
now join me to proudly say
Jai Jai Gyan

Ashok Kini Hosdurg
15 August 2008

FAITH FOUNDATION

An Organisation in India with difference

Faith foundation an inter faith organization formed to protect our UNIVERSE. Every human being taking birth on this home planet EARTH has responsibility to preserve this EARTH and the UNIVERSE.

OUR SLOGAN

We belong to one religion
"Religion of Humanity"
We belong to one family
"Family of Global Society"

Visit : *www.faithfoundation.in*

Global Society

Faith Foundation will work for creation of environmental, educational, medical, Vedic, mythological research institutes, and also create a foundation for humanitarian help with the above research work, dedicated to serving the society.
Inspire and assist students or institutes or individuals to carry out research work on space, environment, medical, education, earth science, ancient science, Vedic, and life force (soul) for good of humanity.
Self purity, soul realization and to create a world of enlightened souls.
Research on use of Astro and Cosmic energies.
Provide Security and help to widows, orphans, old aged and also make the globe beggar-free.
Conduct educational and self-development programs to offer techniques to eliminate stress, improve health, expand awareness and resolve conflict-within.
Assist growth of children and provide education with values, food and shelter for the needy.
To create Global Societies in all the countries across the world under the banner of GLOBAL SOCIETY, a vision of great king Samrat Ashoka. A gift to Global Humanity from India.

SAVE THE EARTH
पृथ्वी की रक्षण कीजिये

पृथ्वी गायत्रि

ॐ पृथ्वी-देवै विद्महे
सहस्रमूर्तै धीमहि।
तन्नो पृथ्वी प्रचोदयात्।।

May we realise Prithvi-Devi, the Mother Earth. Let us meditate on her thousand aspects as Sahasramurti. May Prithvi, the Mother Earth, Illumine us.